THE HOME MODERNISED

Making a home for the way you want to live today

THE HOME MODERNISED

ANDREW WEAVING

with photography by Andrew Wood

jacqui
small

First published in 2005 by Jacqui Small LLP,
an imprint of Aurum Press Ltd,
25 Bedford Avenue, London WC1B 3AT

Text copyright © Andrew Weaving

Photography, design and layout copyright
© Jacqui Small 2005

Publisher   Jacqui Small
Editor   Kate John
Art Director   Ashley Western
Production   Peter Colley

A catalogue record for this book is available from the British Library.

ISBN 1 903221 35 8

2007   2006   2005

10 9 8 7 6 5 4 3 2 1

Printed and bound in China

CONTENTS

THE ESSENCE OF
THE MODERN HOME

Page 6 A Victorian house full of original features, in which tongue-and-groove walls, moulded architrave and trim and sash windows are updated with the addition of classic Scandinavian modern furniture. The steel framed chairs are by Poul Kjaerholm.

1 Custom-made furniture by Bill Mostow for his mother's house gives a uniqueness to this bedroom. Furniture with clean, distinct lines can instantly modernise your home. **2** In a 1960s house in Sarasota, classic pieces of furniture by masters such as Le Corbusier and Mies van der Rohe are placed within the rooms to divide the space.

In the words of Florida-based architect, Gene Leedy, 'the urge to remodel is stronger than the sex drive'. Having updated, extended *and* renovated many of his earlier homes built since the 1950s, he knows what he is talking about. In my experience this is so true. Nearly every house I have worked on over the last twenty years or so, and that I have sold, has been bought by someone who loves it, loves every detail of it, loves the finishes, adores the storage, is eager to move in straight away, and even pleads with me to leave certain items. But when you bump into a previous neighbour who tells you 'they've stripped out that wall of storage', 'they've painted all over your colour scheme' or even exclaim, 'they are putting in a new kitchen', you wonder why the client paid over the odds for the house in the first place, if they still wanted to put their own mark on the place. This is what it all really boils down to: making the house yours, to the point at which you can say, for example, 'Oh, we've chosen these tiles for the bathroom, they were made specially for us in a little pottery in Tuscany.'

Whether you are a do-it-yourself expert or not, this happens at all levels. I have even heard of cases where new owners of brand new apartments have changed fittings, taken out walls and laid new floors. You wonder why they bought the property to begin with!

Looking back, there have always been certain types who have searched high and low for a 'wreck' of a house to do up. Now, with the rundown properties all snapped up, it seems that as long as the house is in the right location for you,

3 Graphic pillows, modern lighting and comfy seating all contribute to the modern home. In this city mews house the ceilings have been stripped bare to reveal the structural elements of the Victorian building.

4 Built-in furniture needs to be well planned and well thought out. Different levels give multi use, for example, organisation and display, as achieved by the array of drawer fronts in this orderly dressing room.

even if it is in great condition, modernising a house to make it work for you is today's lifestyle message. It is quite amazing how many people still go with what they initially see when they look to buy a new residence. I suppose they are buying into a lifestyle, even though, when they finally get the keys, all they are buying are four walls with some fittings, and the leftovers of half a colour scheme of the previous owners. To see past this is quite hard for some people.

Today we can do anything we want in our homes within the guidelines of local authorities regarding the planning issues, and within building regulations regarding safety and construction. However, if you want to move services you can, if you want to make an open-plan space, you can. The first thing to work out is how the overall space will best work for you personally and your family.

When you see in the window of a estate agent details saying 'needs updating', 'in need of modernisation', or being sold 'as is' – what does it mean? It all depends at what level you want to approach the renovation. To some, 'going modern' means that they are going to paint all the walls white, put down a light coloured or natural carpet or lay a wood laminate floor. However, within a warren of small rooms with bad lighting, next to no storage and the wrong furniture, there is more to 'going modern' than a quick lick of paint, even though it will help. Overall, there are different degrees of modernisation. The simple use of colour, finishes, lighting and furniture can drastically change your interior. The reorganisation of the space can revolutionise your home: a bigger living area, an open-plan kitchen/diner, or a wall of storage, can make your home work for you in a much more positive way. Extending your space can give that extra room, floor or level that you require. Whether you extend into the roof, excavate the cellar or build out into the garden, this degree of modernisation can be the most stressful, yet most rewarding when completed.

Even on a very low budget, a few simple elements can produce amazing results. Many people do a lot of work before they move into their new home and can end up changing many things once they move in when they realise that certain elements are not working for them. In my experience, it is crucial to first live within the space, experience the daylight changes, and work out your preferred use for each room.

The interior magazine selection available now is ever increasing, with so many ideas and tips for this and that, and collecting images of things that appeal to you is an important part of any new work you are considering for your home.

Modernising your space depends on your needs: from the type of accommodation involved to the size of the family living there; whether or not you work from home; from the size of your budget to establishing how long you intend to stay put. For example, are you doing the modernisation for yourselves or making the place more desirable for the perspective buyer in the near future? Are you going to work on the home as one unit or are you more concerned with

5 An open-plan staircase of steel and laminated walnut rises to various levels. The glass partition acts as a safety barrier and allows light to flood through to the lower floor. **6** In this remodelled Brooklyn house the lower level has been opened up, and access is via this staircase which also acts as important storage and a wet bar for the entertaining area. The stair treads are stained with Indian ink prior to sealing.

the living, dining and kitchen areas? All these questions need to be considered in the initial planning process to help you get focused and organised.

It also depends on what you have to start with. If the Victorian house you have is full of original features, it would be a shame to remove these elements of character. A mix of old and new works well if done sympathetically. An open-plan space with shuttered windows, fireplaces and perhaps some panelling would be a great backdrop to some of today's modern furniture and lighting. Getting a balance of elements is a very important factor. Whether you have an icon of modern design, such as a Mies van der Rohe Barcelona chair or a new piece of design from IKEA, the balance is what it is all about. The scale of modernisation is also to be noted. Again, in a Victorian house, keeping many

original features and perhaps replacing an internal wall with glass bricks may work, but the lighting would have to be considered, and the way the two periods unite would have to be well defined. More importantly, you need to consider whether or not this installation will add to the overall design, layout and use of the areas in question? To use certain 'modernisations' merely for visual effect can make some spaces very aesthetically pleasing, but really every addition needs to have its use. Of course, if the glass brick wall is going to bring much needed light to an interior hallway, this offers a dual solution, as it is both visually exciting and is an effective way of opening up a dark space.

With the availability of so many off-the-shelf products these days – from places like Homebase, B+Q and IKEA, do-it-yourself is now so much easier. Many stores offer printed

7 The long kitchen island is reminiscent of John Pawson's work. Curtis Wood used Pawson's house as an inspiration for the client. The wall of doors opens up to reveal more work space and storage.

8 In this simply modernised home everything has been painted white – from the floors and walls to the vintage seating arrangement. The light box is left over from a recent exhibition. In this space the areas are divided with simple and effective sliding panels.

instructions of how to do certain tasks, for example, how to replace this and that fitting, how to lay a wooden or tiled floor, how to build a shower cubicle, or even how to build a glass brick wall. In some ways this is a good move forward, in another way it could be potential for disaster. To work on a series of individual areas is not really a good idea. On the whole your home is one unit and to make the modernisation work, it is best to treat it as a whole. Even if it is simply the floor treatments – one type of flooring on at least one level creates a modern feel to the place – it is the start of a total or whole renovation. All the other aspects need to be considered when modernising an interior as a whole, for example, deciding on a colour scheme for the entire space and using lighting that is similar throughout. If you work on a schedule and try to get things done in stages, the whole space will end up as a united modern place in which to live and work.

In some countries, the lack of modern housing has created an enormous interest in making what you have more modern. In a modern house it is usually the layout and room proportions that make the house more modern than, say, a house of an earlier period. Reorganising your home space can make a drastic improvement to a property if it is well executed. There is nothing worse than an open-plan space that has had every wall removed and where the front door opens directly up onto a massive void. Walls are as important as the space around them. In many cases, a wall in the right place can visually create more space. What is behind the wall can also give a feeling of greater space beyond.

The most important part of changing the layout of your space is to understand the construction of what you have. Some walls can be removed without any structural supports, but others that are load bearing need to be reinforced with beams. Advice from a structural engineer may be necessary. For example, in a three-storey house which has four bedrooms, there is the question of the space that has conventionally been used for sleeping. In an inner city environment, it is possible that a family with three or four children would not want to live in this location. As a workable solution to creating more space, maybe more living areas could be modelled from some of the bedroom spaces. In today's property business, even though some estate agents still describe the accommodation as a '4 beds, 2 bath' kind of layout, this is slowly changing; a two-bedrooom house with 2000 square feet of living accommodation sounds so much more appealing and spacious in comparison.

The division of space is what it is all about. In an open-plan living, dining and kitchen area, visual breaks are necessary to define the space. Whether it is with the use of different flooring to demarcate specific areas, full-height screens or partitions to break the view, or lighting elements to create pools of light where necessary, it is important to consider all these elements when gutting and remodelling your home.

To many, extending your home is the ultimate ambition. If you have a large unused roof space, a dark damp cellar, or a large side or rear garden, extending can save you having to move house. Of course, all these projects would need guidance from the appropriate authorities. Certain works are permitted developments, for example, extending upwards to a certain size. Developing the roof space into living accommodation is all about access and ceiling heights, so if you have to raise the roof level you will need to apply for consents. With so many firms now specialising in specific types of extension, the whole process is so much easier. If you want to go for a glass extension, I recommend that you go to the specialists. They will do all the necessary, from the plans to the finished results. These disruptive methods of making your house more modern and increasing your space really only work well when they are well thought out.

It has taken quite a long time to get to this modernisation urge. Not so long ago, it was the fashion that once you had become successful at your work and you had a chance to decorate your home, you would opt for a safe interior of over-stuffed chintz sofas and a few antiques – visual indicators that you had some money and good taste. All of a sudden, there seems to be some kind of competition as to how modern can you make your home. I suppose the reason is that you can look through magazine after magazine at 'so called' modern interiors, but it is only once you have actually been in one, and experienced the space and light, that you you realise how the same look can work for you.

The modern interior is really quite classless – it is a matter of understanding your space, making it work for you and using every square foot of your home for its appropriate use. There are different levels of materials you can use to achieve the same desired effect. A painted concrete floor can give a similar feel to a honed stone floor, sanded and polished floorboards can give similar warmth as an exotic timber floor. It is all about putting many elements together that balance with each other and create a modern harmony. Looking back to earlier examples of the modern interior, many places included the use of very basic materials, which were both easily available and spot on for their use and effect. In the 1930s architects such as Wells Coates and Serge Chermayeff were both commissioned to remodel and modernise city apartments and houses, bringing them up to date with modern furnishings, new layouts and lighting. With extensive building in the US throughout the 20th century, the American modern interior was all part of a way of life. We look to these interiors for inspiration today, for colour schemes and finishes. Mies van der Rohe gave us inspiration for placing furniture within the space while Richard Neutra gave ideas for built-in furniture, recessed lighting and the mix of materials used throughout today's modern interior. Each has its place in the contemporary home.

9 A classic spiral staircase holds its own in its own unique space. The dark painted wall behind adds to its visual impact. **10** In this Florida home, a wood burning fireplace has been installed to create a focal point. Even in the Sunshine State, a bit of extra heat is sometimes needed.

THE HOME TRANSFORMED

Page 18 What were once two neighbouring apartments in neighbouring houses have been knocked together to form one unit. A rare occurrence because since both buildings are owned by the same Co-op they were treated as one through the planning process.

1 A family heirloom – a patchwork quilt – has been made into a curtain. While making a great insulating drape, its visual impact unites the textures and colours used throughout this Helsinki apartment. **2** The Scandinavian 1950s screen-printed linen pillows and the wooden relief panel by Brian Willsher are the only elements of decoration in this grouping. They somehow complement each other. The wall light is one of the original features from the house that has now been restored.

DECORATIVE MODERNISATION

Making your home more modern by the means of simple elements such as paint, wallpaper, new floors, lighting and key items of furniture is the easiest and quickest method. Even if you are renting your space you can achieve amazing results just with a bit of thought, research and time. By taking what you have, changing what is out of date and adding selected modifications, the home you have can be easily updated. Without the need to worry about structural alterations or any major upheaval of day-to-day living and working, decorative modernisation is ideal for those seeking a quick home 'makeover'.

Most of the areas you will be working on can very easily and quickly be altered. The problem in many cases is making the decisions. In past schemes I have worked on, as much as 10 years ago, the choice of modern elements was always quite limiting. Nowadays, wherever you go, whether it be the local hardware store or the home DIY superstores, the range of decorative materials is endless. From lighting to cabinet pulls, from wallpaper to the selection of shades of white paint, the time it takes to decide can be the most difficult of all the procedures to create a modern home.

Where to start is perhaps also one of the difficult tasks. You move into a new home with an out-of-date kitchen, a coloured bathroom suite, various floor coverings, bad lighting and little or no storage. So where do you begin? With this kind of modernisation, as no major alterations are going to be done, it is not so much of a worry. If you paint the bedroom bright red or paper it with

3 In the kitchen/dining area of Karim Rashid's New York loft, the use of optical laminate to face the kitchen cabinets makes these flat planes decorative. The grouping of pots by Sottsass for Memphis adds some colour to this sociable area.

70s wallpaper and then you decide you hate it only after a few weeks, you can simply paint over it or cover it with something else. But I find that if you can experience the space first, for example, noting the light changes and work out the best layout for the room in question, you can try sample colours at different times of the day and a get more of a positive result that way.

Working on the decoration while you are still living out of packing crates is a good time as you can camp out in one room while you work on another.

If you have been in the same place for a while it is rather more difficult to get started. I would suggest that you begin by having a major clear out of all unwanted and useless items that have been collected over the years. With this done, storage is always, in my opinion, the first thing to sort out. In an older property this can often be a problem. However, understair storage can be tidied up and racked with shelving, while alcoves can be fitted with display cubes and low cupboards. Selecting items of furniture that are dual purpose also make this type of modernisation more successful. As one example, beds with under sliding drawers offer very convenient storage.

Whatever type or scale of modernisation you are working on, lighting is one of the most important aspects. In many cases, the installation of a great modern lighting fixture can transform an otherwise dreary room. You can go for total coordinated lighting throughout or just concentrate on the dining area with a re-edition classic.

The placing of great looking furniture gives the ultimate visual impact to a room. Whether selecting from chainstores or hunting out a vintage classic, it is the right piece in the right place that will make the home more modern. Equally, fabrics are a great addition to a modern home as they can be used in a multitude of ways; from adding texture to a bare scheme to bringing tonal harmony to the different elements within the space. Patterned or plain, fabric is an essential companion to today's modern interiors.

The following case studies show how others have taken what they have and added basic elements to achieve a livable and lasting modern space.

4 In Rashid's bathroom, the floor is the reverse of the laminate units. This totally enclosed area is divided from the main living space with a translucent perspex panel.

5 In the child's room of this New York loft, Marimekko prints have been used, bringing colour and pattern to an otherwise unadorned interior.

A TOTAL CONCEPT

Karim Rashid, a New York-based designer of furniture, cosmetic packaging, household goods and interiors, is of Egyptian descent, but is half British. Having designed hundreds of objects for some 400 companies over the past 20 years, Karim Rashid does know what we want. Whether it be a carpet, a lamp, a mirror or a bottle of hand soap, he gets it right. His understanding of the interior is common sense. Rashid has noticed that wherever you go in the world, you see the same stores, consume the same drinks and can buy the same pair of shoes. He says that we seek new experiences in the way we live and use our interiors.

In his own home, which has white floors and walls with wallpaper in selected areas, we see a total concept. The majority of the items in the entire space are designed by him. If he moved to a new location, he could pick up everything and install it somewhere else and it would have the same look and feel. In being featureless – except for the full height windows across the front elevation – this space is ideal for this sort of installation.

The only structural element to the space is the division for sleeping quarters at the far end of the space, and the long rectangle taken out of the length of the main area. This area, which is set aside for the bathroom, cloakroom and utility

areas, does not reach the full ceiling height, therefore the entire visual volume is unaltered. The wall of this space is broken into coloured panels and doors leading to storage areas. The use of colour to highlight this structure accentuates its depth.

Every surface of every object is a different material: from the new stain-free durable textiles to the vinyls and other plastics that are popular today. The lighting – either freestanding or wall mounted – is a statement on its own.

On the whole, this space has been treated as a blank canvas, a space where an entire collection of furniture, furnishings, objects and other items have been put together, where each relates to the next. In one way this can be very extreme but in another, it certainly creates a lasting impact and fresh experience. As no real structural work is part of the visual scheme, the interior can be created very quickly.

3

1 Karim Rashid designed this DJ mixing desk pod for Canadian company Pure Design. Hosting clubs is just another one of his skills. The wallpaper is also by Rashid. **2** A total look installation in his own space showcases the range of products he has designed, from the rug to the seating, from the two-tier tables to the appliqué wall light. The only item not by Rashid is the Bang and Olufsen sound system. **3** In the white box loft space the rectangular area – highlighted by the coloured recess above – houses the bathroom and utility areas. Behind the yellow Plexiglass panel is the main bathroom. The dropped ceiling shows the position of the kitchen and dining area.

SYMPATHETIC RESTORATION

This house was designed by Oliver Hill in 1935. One of what became a large estate of international style housing, this house is just one of the very few that was actually built, and is part of the largest group of individually designed modernist houses in the UK.

Being the first showhouse to have been published at the time of construction, good original photographs have enabled a sympathetic restoration and interpretation of Hill's initial concept. In reading through his archive, information which was found mentioned all manner of design elements and decisions, ranging from paint colours to suitable planting for hedges. In one letter, Hill praised the work of the young architect/designer Alvar Aalto, whose furniture he suggested should be used in the showhouse. This house therefore includes furniture and accessories by Aalto alongside other pieces, also designed and made in the 1930s. It may sound extreme to limit one's selection to a period of design. But in a way, it is common sense, as the scale and design of furniture produced at the same time as the building was looked upon as a way forward. How more modern can you get than a simple white box with simple structured furniture without adornment?

When this house was discovered about five years ago, it had not been inhabited for some years. It had been 'modernised' in the 1950s and then again in the 1970s. Both of these schemes removed original elements and introduced features of those decades. Every surface was covered with patterned wallpapers and carpets. Removing these revealed the original pine parquet floors and plain smooth walls that curve into the ceilings without coving. Doors to balconies and terraces were bricked up and pelmets and tiled ledges adorned the windows.

Now the house has all its original elements. All unnecessary decoration has been removed. Metal framed doors have been installed and shiplike railings on the balconies have been reinstated.

In the main living room, with its 4.5m quarter radius window, furniture has been selected to create an ideal room for entertaining and relaxing. The floors have been stripped and polished. Simple graphic design rugs and furnishing fabrics for pillows have been added and vintage lighting has either been restored or reinstated.

Overall, if you are working on a 20th century modern style home, assess the elements of the period and try to include them into a scheme for today, with vintage furniture and furnishings.

In this 1930s coastal property, the original metal framed strip window curves around the house. The furniture are all period pieces, and yet give the room a contemporary feel. The clean lines of the architecture is complemented in the furnishings. Note how the walls curve into the ceiling.

COLOUR & PATTERN UNITED

In this apartment on the 13th-storey of an old midtown industrial building, you find an installation of colour and pattern put together by the owner Jo Shane, who resides here with her husband and their two children. Being an artist, Jo has a natural instinct of putting the initial concept together. Having a great sense of colour and being able to place items together in a harmonious way is a great gift.

Alongside a selection of family inherited mid-century classic furniture, new pieces of design and craftsmanship from local artisans have been placed. The use of pattern amongst the pure and simple lines of the George Nelson, Charles Eames and Florence Knoll-designed furniture and the interior architecture by Jurgen Rheim of 1100 Architect, gives a balance of scale and impact whilst bringing the otherwise retro look up to date. In the main sitting area, a long sofa by Knoll is positioned alongside the surfboard table by Eames. With both sitting

1 The bed placed along the window wall gives ample space in the room for regular boys' activities. The colour scheme brings a touch of nature to this high rise city location. **2** Classic mid-century furniture is grouped in the relaxing zone. With new rugs and pillows, this retro area is right up to date. The vintage lamp makes the Nelson Coconut chair the ideal place for a quiet read. An Eames surfboard table is an ideal surface for a collection of small treasured objects.

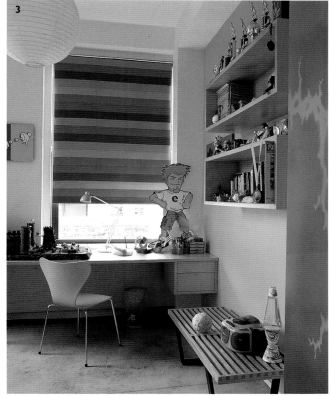

3 The multi tone green room for Jo Shane's son has a built-in desk area for homework sessions. The wall-mounted storage units house both necessary school books and treasured items and trophies. The slatted bench is by George Nelson.

on a modern take on of an ethnic rug and with the equally ethnic embroidered pillows, this area is reminiscent of the Eames's original way of living in their house in Santa Monica. A collection of different cultures and styles alongside modern design elements creates a pleasing effect.

The low level approach is also reflected in the long low bench that runs along the entire length of the apartment. The George Nelson Coconut chair, while being both a great chair chair to sit in and to look at, brings together this sociable and relaxing zone.

The children's rooms are away from the main core of the apartment; the unusual shape of these rooms enables the room to work as both a sleeping zone and a place to work.

The bed along the window wall gives ample space to play and also ample seating when friends come around. The desk provides a great place to do homework and ideally will help instil organisational skills from an early age. Storage and display areas are important for children as it enables them to live, work and play in an organised environment and ensure that they keep their own rooms tidy and have their favourite things on show.

At this high level the apartment doesn't see any treetops, so by using various shades of green in this room, it brings the colour of nature into the son's room. This room also includes useful modern design classics such as the Jacobsen series 7 chair, the Nelson slatted bench and steel cased nightstand.

CLASSIC INTERPRETATION

This loft space in London's docklands near Canary Wharf has been filled with mid-century modern furniture classics.

Using furniture as a decorative way to modernise your home can often be the simplest way to achieve the best result. If you are lucky enough to have a space which only requires a lick of paint, then furnishing the place can result in an almost instant transformation.

Perhaps you are moving from a previous home where you already have some great pieces of furniture and lighting. If not, there are endless outlets for good and interesting pieces, whether by certain designers or not. In this urban space, the majority of items are from the US, including works by George Nelson and Florence Knoll.

As well as looking good, the furniture you select has to work, as space is usually valuable. In this space, a storage system by George Nelson has been installed along the wall of the main living space. This system called CSS – comprehensive storage system – was designed in the late 1950s and developed over a few decades with updates of finishes and hardware. This system was produced in the mid-sixties; it includes drawers, display cabinets, drop-front desk units, book storage and display shelves. It groups everything together using the enclosed areas for organising your life and using the open areas for displaying your collections. On this unit a large selection of wooden sculptures by London sculptor Brian Willsher provide the key focal point.

When this loft space was purchased, the decoration was somewhat personalised by the previous owners. The walls were brick red as were the concrete floors. Now, with the white walls and the painted concrete floors, the space is now a simple environment for well designed furniture to be seen and used. The seating throughout the living area is all designed by Florence Knoll. The classic sofa and occasional chairs still retain their original upholstery.

In this simple makeover, pattern is bought in with graphic pillows by New Yorker Jonathan Adler, and an old striped rug, sourced from a local flea market. A bit of pattern brings scale to the space.

If you are lucky enough to be able to go into a new space that just needs decorating, bear in mind how you want the place to look. It takes more than paint and textiles to make the place yours. You need to add good looking, comfortable furniture and the right kind of lighting that creates both a sympathetic mood for the interior, and highlights the treasures of your home.

2

1 The white painted brick walls act as a great backdrop to the vintage furniture and the skyscraper sculpture. **2** In the main living area off this loft space, a storage unit by George Nelson dominates the area. Here all is hidden away or on display as necessary. The concrete floor is simply painted.

MIX & MATCH

This small apartment is on the upper floors of a turn-of-the-century block, typical of many found in various European cities. The block is set around a communal courtyard for bicycle parking and for hanging washing out to dry. With this space designed by interior architect Ulla Koskinen, simple, complementary decoration has been used to add to the impact of the classic 20th-century furniture; which just proves that modern doesn't have to be brand new.

The apartment consists of two bedrooms, a study, the main living room and a kitchen/dining room. Typical of Scandinavian design, the floors are stripped wood with an opaque whitewash to keep them pale.

In what is predominantly a white interior, primary colours have been introduced, with the use of furniture upholstery and lacquer finishes. The main sitting room area boasts a long low red sofa running under the two windows and a pair of 1930s Aalto big cantilever armchairs, bringing the modern elements to this period apartment.

1 A long low sofa runs the length of the window wall. A deep shelf has been built in to increase the depth for display and unites the two windows.
2 An Alvar Aalto chair brings in some colour to the overall white space. Behind is the original ceramic fireplace. To the left are the double doors to the dining area. This scheme shows how, with the addition of colour to your home, you can bring it up to date while at the same time making the most of its classical proportions.

3 Through the double panelled doors is the kitchen/dining area. The red lacquer table brightens up the monochrome scheme and makes the room less kitchen like. **4** A section of cabinet has been removed to house the television for dinner time viewing. Through the narrow door at the end is the bathroom.

Along the window wall also runs a deep shelf added to the existing ledges that unites the two windows and adds a great area for display, while also disguising the heating elements for the apartment.

This space with its original features is as it was built: panelled doors, skirting boards, moulded ceiling roses and a ceramic corner fireplace. As all these details are painted white they remain subtle yet key elements and provide a solid background for the new elements introduced.

In the kitchen/dining room, a mix of black and white units makes the space more of an extension of the main living area than a kitchen, especially since the cabinets have been made to look more like built furniture. The bright red lacquered table was designed by Ulla Koskinen for this space, and again, brings fresh colour to a monochrome scheme.

Taking what you have and making the most of it is often overlooked when trying to make your home more modern. There is no need to remove period details. Painting everything one colour disguises these features to some extent, but still reminds you that you are in an older surrounding. It is more about what you add than what you take away that makes the space up to date. For example, if the panelled doors had been replaced with flat ones or lower the ceilings with for low voltage down lighters, this space could have become yet another bland 'modern' apartment, void of any soul or character. Instead of which, it has unique modern qualities.

UNIFORMITY OF DESIGN

1 This main living area with its painted floor and furniture is white from top to toe. The red shag pile rug brings in colour. Note the exercise equipment for the frustrated gymnast. **2** Stainless steel fronted kitchen cabinets and appliances work well in this industrial space. The recess used is just the right size for all the necessities. **3** The dining area is divided from the sitting area by the original half glazed wall. The deep beams run through both spaces as do the vintage enamelled pendant lights.

This industrial unit in the Kruununhaka area of central Helsinki was once a knitting factory. Now taken over by creative director Mikko Mannisto, partner Tuula Poyhonen, a fashion designer, and children Mosse, Olb and Ere, it is a simple home for a family with one full-time child and the occasional visit from the others.

This space is all about going back to basics. What you see is what you get. The fairly small space of four rooms with a bathroom is on the ground floor of the 1920s development, originally built for housing businesses in the town centre. Surrounding internal communal gardens, the external space is like a walk back in time. However, once inside it is a different story. You enter a large space divided from the next space by an original half glazed screen wall. The compact kitchen area with its stainless steel faced cabinets creates an industrial feel to complement the utilitarian space. In this small grouping of elements you can find all you need, from stove to dishwasher.

The main space, which makes up the dining area, has a white painted floor. The furniture appears to be discarded office chairs scattered around an old pine table on wheels. The simplicity of all the elements makes it easy to feel at home as soon as you enter. There are no precious furnishings to damage and no precious 'designer' chairs to sit on. It is all child-friendly and complementary to the building's original architectural and decorative features. Floors and walls are painted white, creating a simple backdrop where everything looks good.

The glazed double doors lead through to the main living area with a vintage sectional seating arrangement, painted white with white upholstery. Off to the side lies the simple sleeping area – a futon and a storage facility on wheels – reached via a sliding partition. The only colour found in the entire space is introduced with the use of throw rugs – a rag rug for the kitchen and a red shag rug for the living area.

Between the deep beams in these rooms hang what look like original enamelled steel pendant lamps. Using the same fittings throughout unites the spaces; a uniformity of design and period is always important. Retaining so much originality gives the space soul and a firm footing. On a modern note, the dividing partition adds a great feature; it demarcates the zones and with windows on both sides, adds to the ease of organisation here with both sides being well lit.

Overall, this type of space works when you take into consideration what there is to start with. Using decoration to make your existing space more modern is the simplest way to achieving an almost instant transformation, whatever the original style or type of accommodation.

3

UPDATING FEATURES

In any type of property, some original features will exist, while some will have been completely removed. The last house I lived in had been updated in the 1970s. All the features except the dog-leg staircase had been removed. So we put in a new modern staircase. The new straight flight of stairs created more space in the hallway and instantly united the modern kitchen area with the open-plan living area.

Being as lucky as this is quite hard to come by now. With older, more intact houses being in such demand in recent years, even if a Victorian house was missing some original details, they most probably would have been reinstated by now. In some cases you could be taking on a project that could involve a combination of removing and updating reproduction features.

The best way to start is to take note of what features exist, what features you want to keep or restore, and what features need to be updated. It is important to get a good balance of original and new features.

Keeping or reinstating the elevation of the house always works well as it gives the house its architectural balance of window space and masonry. Inside the room these windows give the correct balance of light and proportion to the space. If you intend to keep a few features it is always best to retain the most original features, even if these are not completely intact or in pristine condition. A great cornicing and skirting board acts as a fantastic backdrop to a large abstract canvas.

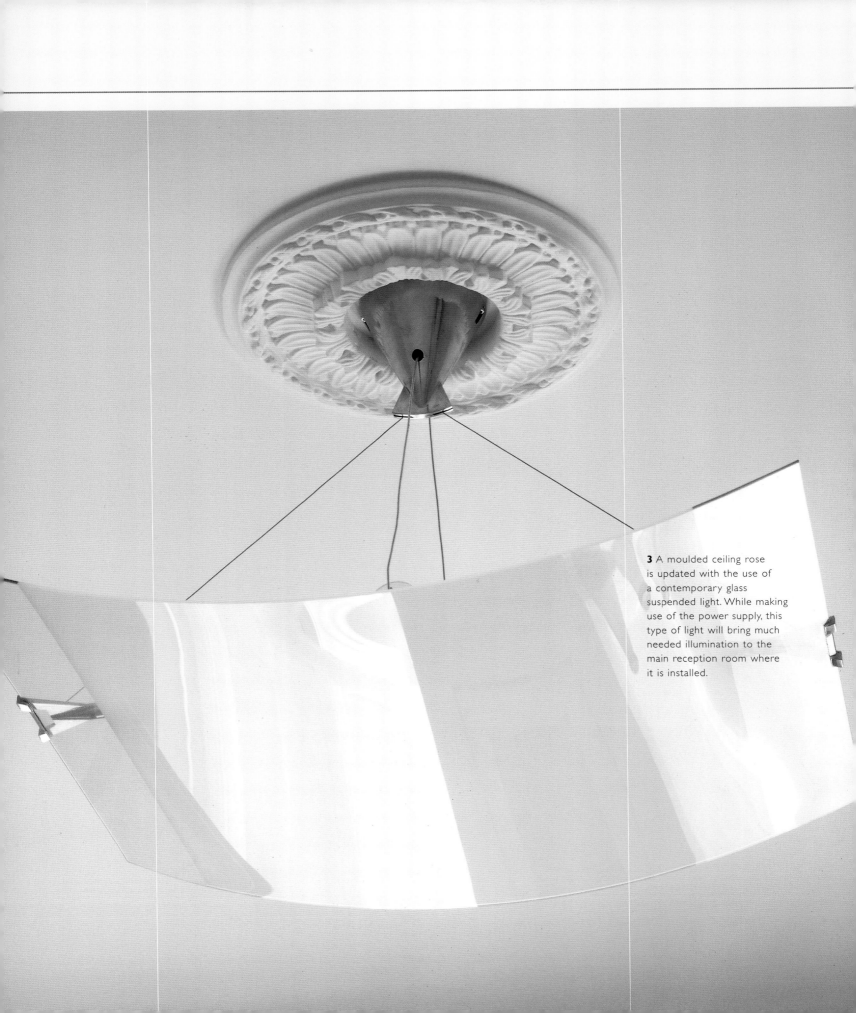

3 A moulded ceiling rose is updated with the use of a contemporary glass suspended light. While making use of the power supply, this type of light will bring much needed illumination to the main reception room where it is installed.

Removing mouldings and cornicing can be a lengthy and expensive job. Sometimes in conversions you may get half of a ceiling in one room and the other half next door. Taking them down will of course give a new feel to the room and remove the obvious signs of an earlier alteration.

The focal point of the main room will often be a fireplace. A simple marble surround can be updated with a simple grate. However, removing it completely can sometimes make the room appear quite bland. Keeping something there as a focal point is perhaps the most important element, and even a hole in the wall can look effective.

Sometimes the changing of simple things like the height of doors to rooms can dramatically modernise the space. Changing conventional doors to sliding panels can be even more radical and provide much more space. Equally, the unification of floor covering can give a great feeling of space and modernity. If you are lucky enough to have a great original floor, make the most of it and restore and repolish it. In many cases, floors are patched up and cut up. The easiest way to improve this is to install a new surface over the existing level with a new or reclaimed material that follows through from room to room. With so much choice available, ranging from massive wide oak planks, to poured resin, there are many options available. This is likely to be the most instant way of updating your space as it unites the spaces and gives a simple background to whatever you add to make this space your modern home.

Sometimes features need to be removed when they dominate the scheme you are working on. This is especially true in reclaimed industrial spaces. Some structural features give great character to a place, but if you want a simple up-to-date space, a series of structural beams and trunking can be unsightly. Lowering areas of ceilings to disguise these elements can also discreetly house lighting and sound systems.

Overall, updating features of your home can be interpreted in many ways. One option is keeping everything in its place but changing its appearence and finish. Repositioning the focal elements can not only give great effect but also make the layout appear to have been altered, giving it fresh visual appeal.

The case studies in this chapter cover many aspects of updating, ranging in scale and budgets.

4 Retaining the original features such as the newel post and turned banisters reminds you that you are in a Victorian townhouse. Under the stairs, where the old dark bathroom lay, the compact space has been transformed into a bright glazed shower room. Alongside leads to the kitchen. **5** This room within the centre of the Old School House has had one of its doorways filled with glass blocks. While bringing a modern element, it also allows an expanse of light into the living area.

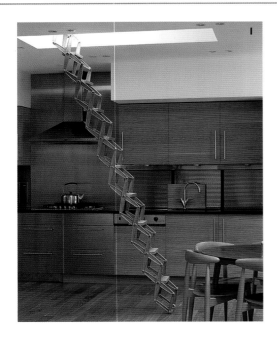

1 In the open-plan kitchen a folding ladder allows access to the much needed outdoor space of this urban mews house. When not in use it can be pushed up into its recess. **2** Some of the exposed elements of the roof structure are visible above this kitchen space. The stools and high table create a handy area to perch for breakfast. **3** The kitchen is installed along the back wall of the house. Being open plan to the rest of the space, it needs to fit in visually with the surrounding features. Using timber doors to the cabinets ties in with the flooring and stairway details found on this level. The dining set includes a set of three-legged chairs by Hans Wegner.

This is a typical mews house, which, from the exterior, looks small like a 2-up-2-down cottage. What must have originally been the garages are now the ground floor bedrooms, creating an upside-down house.

On entering the main living and relaxing area on the upper level, you realise that the house has a wing at the back that doubles its imagined volume. Originally it would have most probably been a warren of smaller rooms. Now it is treated as one space.

The L-shaped floor plan divides the space naturally so that the kitchen area spreads across the back wall, so that when you are relaxing in the entertaining area, it is not visible.

The main feature of this house is that the ceilings and some of the walls have been stripped back to their basic construction materials. The house has been updated by creating a loft-like space. With the bare rafters and beams and the exposed brick work, the house feels like an industrial or agricultural building. In contrast, for example, in the kitchen, new plaster has been applied to give a slick and contemporary feel.

There is a good balance of old and new in this house. Only the dividing wall to the next door house has been stripped of its plaster. This wall includes one of the two fireplaces on this floor. The fireplace in the kitchen/dining area has a small period wood burning stove. In the main

4 Within the roof structure, skylights have been installed to bring more light into the centre of the open-plan space. They are screened here with a blind system on pulleys to diffuse the overhead midday sun. **5** The staircase comes up directly from the lower level into the main living space, alongside the brick feature wall that carries on down the stairs. There are various skylights throughout the roof, bringing natural light to the whole space. The stair surround becomes a natural display area.

relaxing area, a contemporary firehood stove has been installed, replacing the original. This really updates this area, and, with the shag pile rug, gives the impression of a movie set from the 70s.

Skylights have been installed in strategic places in the roof to bring light into the central areas of the reception floor. Blinds to the skylights cut out the overhead sunlight.

Throughout the house there is a mixture of vintage and contemporary designed furniture and accessories. In the kitchen, a Hans Wegner dining set sits alongside a pair of vintage fireside chairs. Using a mix of new and old can give your home an instant 'lived in' look. Vintage pieces give soul

to a new interior and bring individuality to a modern environment. With so many of today's interiors aspiring to look the same, it is prudent to spend time looking for more unique pieces of furniture to achieve a unique look for the home.

This house has been updated simply by removing the decorative finishes applied to the construction materials. Revealing brickwork and timbers gives a certain look and you need to be careful to avoid it giving the space too much of a rustic feel. By making just one feature wall of brickwork shows the structure of the house without dominating the overall contemporary feel of the space.

Architect Anne Fougeron lived in this house for many years before deciding what to do with it. She loved the Victorian house with its handcrafted turned features. So she decided to work with what she had and make the most of the proportions and details. Throughout the house good simple modern design elements are put together successfully with the original aesthetics of the old house.

Fougeron didnt want to turn this house into another contemporary makeover. Taking note of what the house had to offer, she recognised that the areas that needed help most were the dark hallway bathroom and the featureless back of the house. Restricting all the modernisations to the original footprint of the house enabled Fougeron to keep all the original services in their existing positions, even though the electrics and plumbing were updated at this time.

The original kitchen always lacked that inviting appeal that you would expect from a family kitchen in this kind of house. Removing the back wall and replacing the gridwork of the old windows with laminated sheets of glass opened the kitchen up completely to the outside terrace. While instantly visually increasing the size of the room it also bought the

BEFORE LEFT
Beyond the main living rooms is a selection of smaller divided rooms, including a small bathroom with a seperate WC. The kitchen includes a walk-in storage area.

AFTER BELOW LEFT
A new shower room has been installed that juts out from the existing flank wall, thus giving a greater floor area to the kitchen space. The solid walls between these rooms have been replaced with glass.

1 The kitchen, still in its original location, has had its back wall completely removed, opening up this entire space to the outside via a totally glazed wall. **2** The central kitchen island houses the cooker top. This is the hub of the household with the barstools making an ideal place to sit and socialise. On the left is the glass wall of the shower room.

3

4

3 & **4** The fully glazed shower room has a transclucent glass wall onto the kitchen. The recessed strip light glows green at night.
5 The well fitted shower room has a built in stainless steel vanity unit, recessed storage and ample mirrors. The terrazzo floor butts up to the existing oak strip floor that has been bleached and polished.

outside in and opened up the back of the house to provide great views of the neighbourhood beyond.

Using a minimal steel frame with the glass mounted with clear silicon, the plane of glass is almost uninterrupted.

The floor standing units are complemented by the central cooking and eating island, making this area the core of the house where everyone can gather.

The hallway bathroom lies alongside the kitchen. Previously a narrow, dark room, this space is now filled with light achieved by installing laminated glass in framed panels, which mimick the full-height windows in the kitchen.

This new shower room is accessed from beneath the ornate Victorian staircase. This bathroom is treated as a complete wet room with its terrazzo floor and gully for drainage. There is also spacious built-in sink area and concealed steel faced storage cabinets. At night the opaque glass is illuminated by a subtle neon light.

The works took about 12 months to complete and in this time Fougeron was able to try new products and include well tested techniques from her previous projects.

From the front of the property, it is hard to tell what size the house is and what its layout is. This house is very deep. The first floor consists of a large living room and a dining hallway which leads onto the kitchen at the back of the house where the terrace has access by a spiral staircase to the garden below. In these rooms, classic pieces of modern design which work well with in the classic proportions of this historic house, are found.

5

materials and styles. Keeping to a more uniform colour and material helps unify the spaces.

In the relaxing zone, the spiral staircase to the upper floors has been retained, but nothing else. The fireplace, which extended much further into the room with brick piers and a copper canopy, has been updated with the strikingly plastered and painted chimney breast and storage of logs. Throughout the space are iconic pieces of design, for example the Arco lamp, now being reissued, which arches across the space.

The door at the end of this room leads to the original entrance lobby – partially divided with a wall of glass bricks – and the original heavy front door. Through the entrance lobby is the kitchen, the focal point of which is the original extractor hood, giving the cooking area a permanence. At the end of the kitchen, full height windows open out to the courtyard. These doors and windows were originally painted black. They have been spray painted white and now look as modern as the whole kitchen.

This old school house has seen many transformations in its lifetime. Originally a Victorian village school, it has since been a public house, a tea room and various other establishments in between. The layout of the house has been added to and extended over the years and consists of the original school hall with the head teacher's office off that and a one-storey extension off to the side and back of the house. Now it has been saved by its new owners, Angi Lincoln and John Orum, who have tackled the lengthy job of clearing out the old and introducing the new.

The ground floor now consists of a large reception room with a spiral staircase to give access to the floor above, a central kitchen that unites the areas, a study room, and various other rooms for activities such as working out or painting. Three bedrooms, a dressing room and large bathroom occupy the upper level.

Many features that the owners inherited have been updated. The flooring finishes throughout have been changed and upgraded: from the tongue-and-groove plywood panels in the kitchen hallway, to the laminate strip in the relaxing zone. Previously there was a whole array of

3

1 The focal point, the fireplace is fully working, but also acts as summer storage for logs when not in use. The cowhide rug provides some pattern and texture and the Arco lamp brings the school house up to date, even though it was designed in the 1960s. **2** Using the industrial looking extractor duct work from the old kitchen gives the new cooking area a professional look. Light floods in from the courtyard at the end of this space. **3** The existing entrance to the house still retains its old oak front door. This area has been modified to include a cloakroom divided from the original space by a glass brick wall.

COOL AND FRESH SPACES

1 The old kitchen cabinets have been faced with white laminate to update them. The wooden walls and ceiling have been painted white and the floor has been refinished with brick pavers. **2** In the large master bedroom, a large ensuite shower room makes the space feel complete. The full height sliding doors give access to each side of the house as well as adding a natural cooling effect.

In this 1950s post-and-beam house in Florida, the entire space was initially updated and modified by the original architect, Gene Leedy, and since then by its new owner Robert Kaiser. From its original plan it has been slightly extended, so that what was once two bedrooms is now one.

This house was originally quite obviously a timber frame house, as early photographs show the walls to be polished veneered ply and the ceilings tongue-and-groove cedar. Also the floors originally comprised cork squares.

Fifty years on from its construction, the house is now as modern as it was when first built. The almost transparent aspect between the interior space and the outer area surrounding the property is apparent due to a series of sliding glass doors. Visually, these create a seamless blend of architectural features – for example, directly outside the bedroom is

a new pool, installed by Kaiser. Across from the pool a guest house provides relaxed accommodation for friends and family.

In the main house, the original cork floor has been replaced with a brick one. Laid in an alternate bond pattern it relates to the concrete block used elsewhere around the house. This flooring runs the entire length of the house, thus treating the space as a whole, and offering colour, texture and a cool surface. Likewise, within the whole space, the walls and ceilings have been painted white, helping to brighten up the house.

The kitchen has also been updated. Once a wooden faced kitchen, it has now been faced with white laminate. The bank of original wall cabinets on the back wall have been replaced with modern horizontal steel framed cabinets. Also in this area the original louvered, jalousie, windows have been replaced with sliders.

These offer ideal access for serving drinks directly outside.

In the bedroom area of the house there used to be two double bedrooms divided by a wall of storage. With this partition removed, the space becomes one. Perhaps a luxurious use of space, but with the guest house across the way, there ample is accommodation for visitors. One of the two bedrooms had its own ensuite bathroom. Now the large master bedroom uses this as a shower room. Full height wardrobes run the length of the new bedroom space. This room now has sliding doors at both ends, allowing the space to be exposed to the sun both morining and evening, and, when open, the cross breezes help cool the room during the hot spells.

This house shows that an older space that was so modern when first built can easily be updated to be even more modern than originally intended.

1 The kitchen area in this house consists of a walkway from the living to the dining area. A wall of storage unites all the appliances while the free-standing partition wall acts as a visual break and provides its own wall of hidden storage. **2** The ensuite shower room in this loft apartment is divided by a wall of glass. The wet area floor is concrete while a timber floor covers the rest of the space.

REORGANISING YOUR SPACE

Space is important, but its organisation is even more so. Taking the overall space of your home, removing all existing walls and partitions and reconfiguring the area as a whole is the way to get everything you want in the correct place for today's way of living.

If you have a blank canvas to work with, reorganising the space can be quite a task. Where do you start? How open plan do you want it to be? What do you need to include in the layout? What is your budget? What is the look you are going for? What are your priorities? How many sleeping spaces do you need? How big do you want the kitchen to be? I have always found that to first live in the space is always a good start. But while you are experiencing the original layout, you also need to have some idea of how you perceive the space changing for the better. Good basic construction and knowing what you want are valuable factors in establishing what your options are, so your first consideration should be to call in structural engineers and discuss with the local planning department what you can and cannot do.

When reorganising the space you need a list of requirements. How much storage do you want? What about focal points, display, and specific areas for furniture and artworks you perhaps own already? If you are creating a complete new layout, you have no excuse for bad use of the space; to discover after a reorganisation that you have nowhere to put anything; to leave the existing poor lighting where it is, or to not plan enough storage.

In some projects I have worked on, some of my clients' ideas have not been thoroughly thought out. Sometimes the idea of creating your own space by changing the layout gives people the idea of their home being completely open plan. I've always found that this never really works. With a total open-plan space, there is never anywhere to put anything, every aspect of the space is in constant view, and on a practical level, it can be hard to organise the services. However, the installation of a partition in the correct place can make an area feel twice the size, and one is immediately curious to know what lies behind the wall. The division of a space with a partition of double-sided storage always seems to work well when working out the space layout and storage options.

To some extent, the end result is under some constraints from the original format. If you are working on a Victorian terraced house you can remove walls, relocate the staircase and change the layout. The idea of moving the bedroom areas to the ground floor and the reception upstairs works well for some people, since it might provide a more spacious living area, especially if you open up the roof space. It all depends on your lifestyle. With any terraced house, the width of the house does limit the new layout. Windows which are positioned only at the front and back of a property do create a railroad effect. This results in some rooms without windows being sandwiched between other spaces. Reorganising the space can compensate for this but the planning department may see this differently. It would all depend what the rooms in question are to be used for, and there would need to be adequate light and good ventilation.

In a flat or an apartment, it is sometimes much easier to be successful in reorganising the space. A purpose-built unit would generally have many windows and therefore you can plan the reorganisation so that each designated area has access to a windows and services where necessary.

The industrial space which may comprise a shell apartment gives you a clean slate and this poses its own challenges. Personally, I find it easier to remove and relocate elements than to put up a wall in a completely empty space. In some ways, the ideal end result would be a space with a lot of flexibility, in which the dynamic changed

2

according to the combination of moveable partitions, sliding walls and versatile furniture within.

With many of us working from home now, to have a small area that can be a home office during the day and extra sleeping space when needed is an increasingly popular option. Including this type of work space is always an added bonus to any home. In a regular home layout, a total room allocated to a working space would be wasted space. So configuring how best to include this type of office should be one of the key items on your list of priorities.

The spaces in the following case studies include houses, conversions and industrial spaces.

HISTORIC MEETS MODERN

1 The new stair tower is clad with copper sheet. This area was once the side alley to the existing house. **2** The new stairwell has been relocated to the original position of the side alley of the old house, therefore using this otherwise useless space and allowing for complete open levels within the new floor plan. The pivoting copper clad door opens onto the paved outdoor area.

Besides creating a modern home, this project – by architectural firm Curtis Wood – has entailed renovating a historic façade, reinstating missing period details, constructing a new building and extending the original floor plan.

Located on the riverbank, this Edwardian house had been lived in by the previous owners for many years. It was once a warren of small rooms with leaking roofs and even boasted its own lift shaft. The idea to tear down the old house and rebuild behind the original façade was eventually the best option as not only was the house in very bad condition but working this way would save extra expense due to the fact that no VAT would be payable on such a refurbishment.

The idea to make each floor as open as possible came together when the decision was made to build a stair tower away from the main part of the house. This tower would be positioned in the original alleyway at the side of the house. The copper cladding to the tower would identify it as a new addition to the existing house and would be the embellishment to the otherwise unadorned house, except for the original features on the Edwardian façade.

Inspired by John Pawson's work, the owners of this house did not want the interior to be too clinical. The materials chosen – limestone for the ground floor, oak for the other floors and staircase, and walnut for all the built-in furniture – are complemented by the owners' interest in modern furniture. In the main living area, situated on the ground floor, there are large leather sofas from the 1970s, a pair of 1950s' Italian armchairs – upholstered in velvet – and the occasional free-standing floor light; while much of the lighting is concealed, the architects realised the effect of free-standing lighting in these areas.

The new house behind the façade consists of three floors of accommodation with a large roof terrace, accessed by a continuation of the main staircase within

3 In the kitchen John Pawson's ideas of keeping everything out of sight is adhered to. This wall of storage houses all the kitchen appliances, utensils and crockery. The ground floor, now rebuilt, spans completely from the front through to the rear of the house. A new structural system had to be installed to allow for such open areas. The open-plan sitting area leads into the kitchen space and beyond to the dining zone. An open fireplace runs along the left-hand side of the sitting area. The stairwell is just visible. The furniture is vintage mid-century.

4 From the galley-type kitchen, the open plan space leads to the dining area. The glass wall can be completely opened, enlarging this area to the boundary wall of the rear garden. A limestone floor carries on throughout the entire ground floor. **5** The concertina doors run along a concealed track and fold against the interior wall. There is one slender support at the corner that supports above, enabling all the glass to be opened. The concealed curved track is for the drapery.

5

AFTER ABOVE
The new open plan floor plan shows the new location of the staircase. The kitchen wall storage divides the space, while leading your eye through to the dining area beyond.

the copper clad tower. The ground floor consists of the main sitting area, the kitchen space and a dining extension that completely opens up to the outside area. On the first floor is a more formal sitting room with a full length fireplace and a walnut-faced built-in area that conceals the entertainment equipment; a bathroom, and a small bedroom. The top floor contains the main bedroom with an entire wall of walnut storage, a shower room with glass roof *à la* Pawson, and a further bedroom. Throughout the house, ideas from

Pawson's work can be noted – 'the idea to hide all' – the concealed lighting, the slab-like kitchen island and low-level bench along the fireplace wall. This is an extreme way to reorganise space within your home. It shows the importance of retaining the original façade within the terrace of Edwardian houses. It works on the principle of relocating the staircase to open up the floor plan. With its mix of hard and soft materials, a timeless modern home has been created that will be a solid backdrop for the owners to grow into for many years.

TWO INTO ONE

What was originally two small apartments have been united to produce an attractive and practical duplex. The two 50-metre square spaces have been knocked together to create a modern and compact home.

This approach to creating the ideal home entails stripping bare the original spaces and installing a completely new layout with what you want where you want it. As this space was originally two units it had two kitchens and two bathrooms. Built around 1900, the building was one of the first residential developments of the extension of Amsterdam's inner city. Now it is considered as being the very heart of the city.

The two spaces are pulled together by the installation of the new steel staircase that is placed in the centre of the units and breaks through from one floor to the next. Originally this area was the sleeping zone of the lower space. A large 3-metre square void has been made at this position and creates a massive volume of space.

This now large one-bed duplex has its main relaxing space on the upper level at the opposite end to the bedroom area. Back on the lower level, as you enter you come across a wall of translucent-door storage that in turn via a slightly raised level opens into a large bathroom that is conveniently positioned in the footprint of the previous one.

GROUND FLOOR ABOVE LEFT
What were two apartments is now one duplex. The ground floor was originally a long railroad-type space divided with a a glazed-in bedroom area. The first floor apartment was patitioned into two spaces.

FIRST FLOOR ABOVE RIGHT
The installation of the central staircase unites the two levels; the kitchen, dining and work areas are on the ground floor while the bedroom and main living area is on the upper level.

The kitchen is located in the centre of the overall space opposite the entrance area, and leads into the dining area that includes a traditional approach to the fireplace. From the dining area French doors lead onto a small terrace. These doors and windows add proportion and order to the original framework of the house. An open tread staircase keeps the space free flowing and appears to hover within the void. This staircase with its simple zig zag steel profile structure rises from the raised platform up to the living and sleeping areas.

One of the few walls left standing carries on up from the lower to the upper levels. It is plywood faced and acts as the main division of the space. A study and bedroom are placed behind it. Both rooms also have full-height sliding doors to close off these areas when necessary. The living/relaxing zone on the upper level takes you away from the kitchen and dining area below, and utilises the space available to its best advantage. Today, more social areas are taking preference over large bedroom and bathrooms. The open-plan approach of this space means that the living areas are both accessible and highly usable. With ample storage in the entrance lobby the entire space is clutter free and streamlined.

The materials used – oak floors, steel staircase, white painted walls and kitchen – the use of polycarbonate sheeting for the storage area and the figured plywood for the partition wall creates a simple overall united space.

STREAMLINED MODERN

This 19th-century depot, once used for horse and carriage- and trams was converted into a school in the 1920s, and, after being initially developed into private apartments in the mid 1990s, has more recently been transformed by architect Marc Prosman.

Original features from its previous life are evident on the ground floor of this building. The massive timber beams date from the initial depot's construction. These huge supports give a scale to the entire space and show how one can successfully balance the old with the new, when developing an older building; it is important to create a visual harmony. Using original structures as dividing elements of a space both highlights and incorporates them into the new scheme while avoiding restricting the overall interior and without allowing them to dominate the interior.

The previous layout consisted of a mish mash of unusual shaped rooms with diagonal walls and narrow openings.

2

1 From the central lobby, the screen printed double swing doors open onto the lower level of the living area. The travertine floor carries on through. The high level windows above the kitchen area give ample light without the worry of being overlooked. **2** Looking from the raised level sitting area, the study area is visible. The full-height veneered partition is the identical thickness to the main timber structure beam. The kitchen elements, designed by John Pawson, appear to be moveable within the space. The window at the end overlooks the apartment's garden.

On entering the apartment from the communal entrance, you come upon the bedroom and bathroom areas. All these spaces have been reorganised into streamlined rooms, each kitted out with ample storage and bathroom areas. Keeping all the main services in their original places speeds up the renovation process as you do not need to lay new pipework and plumbing facilities.

From the inner lobby are double silk screened glass doors which lead into the main living space.

BEFORE BELOW LEFT
A warren of strangely angled rooms with what seem to be rooms within rooms. Original features such as columns are well exposed.

AFTER BELOW RIGHT
With most internal walls either moved or removed, the new plan is streamlined. The kitchen and bathrooms remain where they were, enabling an easier and quicker renovation. With the use of sliding partitions every area is usable, but can be enclosed when necessary.

The space in this apartment has been juggled around to make a home that is both flexible and precise and that is a timeless in modern design. **3** On entering the living space from the interior hallway, the openness of the apartment is apparent. Almost every element appears to be moveable. The desk chair on wheels is by Arne Jacobsen. **4** The track of the pocket door is hung from the original structural beam. This door slides into the dividing partition between the kitchen and the study areas. **5** In the study, a custom-made desk makes the ideal work station. There is a pocket door within the full-height partition. The massive beam runs right through the apartment.

Utilising the existing raised level in the main part of the apartment adds another dimension to the relaxing zone. With the cooking, eating and relaxing areas consisting of an open-plan layout, the entire space is treated as a whole. The kitchen has been designed by John Pawson for this apartment and carries on the simple solid design elements of the interior. With white marble in the bathrooms, timber for the dividing screens and walls, and travertine for the floors, these elaborate details bring a fresh dimension to the otherwise traditional materials. Across from the kitchen area is the study area that leads to one of the bedrooms. The dividing wall to the study area is a timber faced structure that is the same thickness as the massive structural beams. It also conceals a pocket door so this area can be closed off when necessary. A wall that is not full height divides the study from the bedroom beyond. This wall of storage houses all work necessities on the study side, while on the bedroom side it houses a plasma screen.

Almost every wall of this apartment has a dual purpose, providing either a screen from another area, a wall of storage or cabinets, or full-height sliding or pivoting doors. This enables the apartment to be opened up and for one space to lead seamlessly to another, while also creating intimate zones for a modern home.

This end of the space has two Vladimir Kagan-designed daybeds, a grouping of Noguchi lamps and two Brancusi inspired ceramic tables. Nothing is built in so all the items are moveable to enable the space to be used for other functions, for example, a sleepover space. With the screens entirely closed this area becomes a translucent box within the space.

The screens slide and fold and when not in use park against the wall in an alcove. The system glides smoothly and makes for easy and quick partitioning. They of course can be left in various configurations to suit the ocasion.

This enclosed space has windows onto the front paved garden. With the original shutters and ironwork this reminds you of the age and style of the townhouse. This lower level still has access to the street, so is even better for guests, who can come and go without disturbing the main household.

Reorganising the space you have in your home enables you to work out what you really need, what you want where and means you can open up unused spaces, thus giving you access to every square foot of your home. It also lets you reassess your total living space and enables you to turn your existing home into a modern living experience for yourselves and your family.

In the lower level of this house, extended and reorganised by architects Ogawa Depardon, the owners wanted to create a family room for the children to play in and in which the family could relax. It is also the main eating area and offers enough space at the front of the house to accommodate the occasional guest.

Once a rental unit with a network of rooms, the entire space has been opened up. The central part has a sinuous deSede sectional sofa, a display area for favourite artworks and oak faced built-in storage for the plasma screen TV and all the accessories.

The flexibilty of this floor is what makes it work. There is plenty of room for the entire family to be able to relax, work or play, all in the same area. The fact that this floor also opens out onto the rear garden just adds to its success. The ingenious installation of the folding screens at the front of the house gives a further dimension to this lower level.

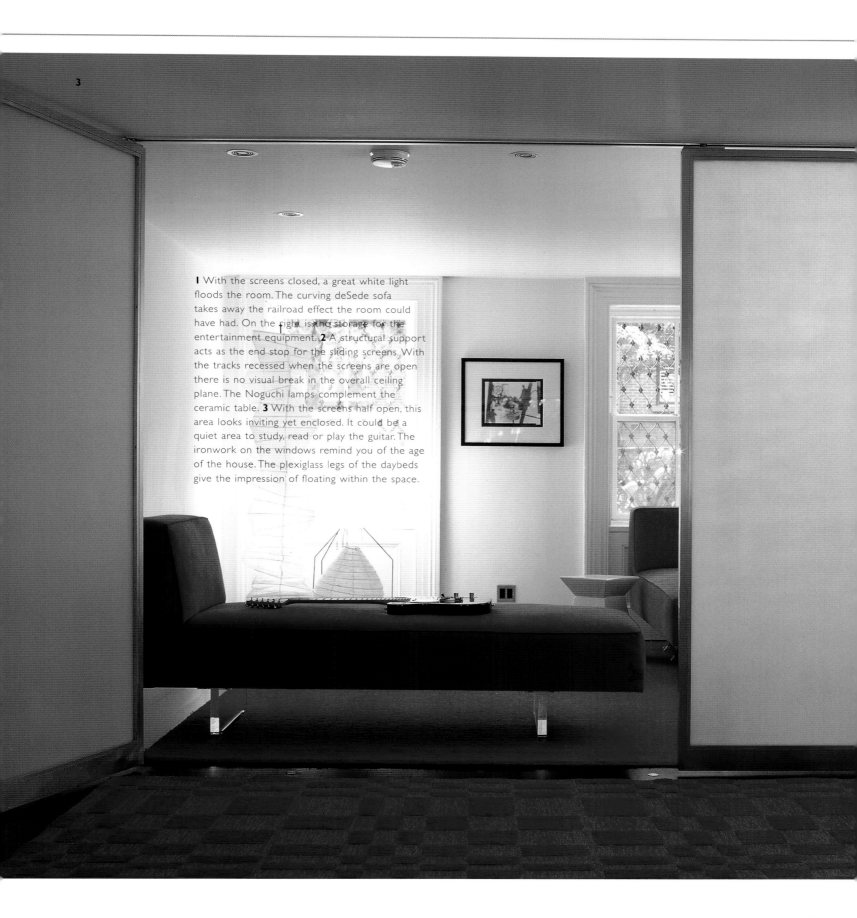

3

1 With the screens closed, a great white light floods the room. The curving deSede sofa takes away the railroad effect the room could have had. On the right is the storage for the entertainment equipment. **2** A structural support acts as the end stop for the sliding screens. With the tracks recessed when the screens are open there is no visual break in the overall ceiling plane. The Noguchi lamps complement the ceramic table. **3** With the screens half open, this area looks inviting yet enclosed. It could be a quiet area to study, read or play the guitar. The ironwork on the windows remind you of the age of the house. The plexiglass legs of the daybeds give the impression of floating within the space.

SPACIOUS FAMILY LOFT

AFTER RIGHT
The plan appears to be a free-flowing circular solution with a central hub of the kitchen and bathroom around the existing building's staircase. The children's rooms are allocated to the angled rooms away from the parents' zone. Lifts open into the apartment's lobby area.

An urban loft has been reorganised for the use of a conventional family set up: mum, dad and their two children.

After moving from a smaller space in a similar area, the owners Jo Shane and John Cooper brought with them a collection of family hand-me-downs, consisting of important design pieces – these range from Eero Saarinen's womb, to George Nelson's Coconut chairs. All of these needed space and prompted the overall direction of the interior.

Taking the unit of over 2500 square feet, the firm 1100 Architect have created a unique modernised space; while including the industrial elements such as the beams, the sprinkler systems and the original concrete floors, they have added slick new features such as the wide walnut floorboards, the sliding translucent doors and partitions and the use of wood effect laminates in the utility areas, including the kitchen.

The whole area is split up into various elements. The central core includes the open-plan kitchen which is flanked with storage behind opaque glass screens (which can be illuminated at night), and pull-out units in the faux walnut wall that back onto the children's wing.

On the west side of the apartment, a complete wall of windows houses the 'den' area – raised slightly off the original concrete slab – comprising a dining area, a living area and a small home office. The slightly different level and flooring materials make this room feel more enclosed and invitingly intimate.

1 With the screens to the den closed, the dining area feels more enclosed and the den becomes a separate unit within the entire space. The George Nelson crossed-leg dining table and the Harry Bertoia dining chairs give a solid design statement to the overall space. The Nelson-inspired bench creates a sense of proportion. **2** With the open screens offering access to the den, the area becomes welcoming and useful. The slightly raised floor level keeps it within its boundaries, yet makes for an inviting space. The wall of storage houses the book collection. The Saarinen womb chair and rare ottoman are both family heirlooms.

With its concrete worktop, the kitchen island acts as the hub of the apartment. The Bertoia barstools are solid yet see-through. The translucent screens on the back wall slide away to expose ample shelving for the useful and precious collection of pots and pans. The faux walnut wall includes pull-out storage and flip-down work areas. The hanging lights are by Biproduct. **4** The master bedroom faces north. The slatted storage bench runs along this room, as in the living areas. The sliding storage area offers yet more storage, this time for clothes. At a high level the sprinkler system is well exposed. **5** The dresssing room that backs onto the master bedroom brings light into the walkway. The hanging clothes create an ever-changing colour backdrop to this area. The fact that this area is on a raised floor gives it feelings of suspension and moveability.

5

4

Along the entire length of this open living, dining and working space runs a window bench which also works as a necessary storage unit.

The master bedroom is placed behind the dressing room that in addition to being the walk-in wardrobe brings light to the walkway, from the main entrance of the apartment to the living areas. This bedroom, on the north side of the building includes an ensuite shower room and has access to a small terrace. The space here has been planned so that the children have their own spaces that are detached from those of the adults who also have their own bathroom.

This loft apartment also includes an art studio with direct access to the elevator and also to the living accommodation. This working zone can be included in the whole space seamlessly yet without interferring with the overall communal living areas.

The reorganisation of space in this house shows, with a balance of the original elements – the introduction of new finishes, the undertaking of the overall demands of the owners and the use of existing furniture and furnishings – how easy, flowing and comfortable a space like this can be.

1 Through the original opening to the old bathroom one approaches the new kitchen. Using services already in place from the previous use of this space makes a simpler installation. **2** The new kitchen, with its island, is raised up on a floating floor. This allows for pipework and electrics to be installed where needed and divides this space from the main living area.

In this ex industrial space the entrance level has been reorganised to make the place more usuable. Originally, you entered a small lobby which opened onto an internal hallway with more doorways, one to an enclosed kitchen and the other to a bathroom. The bathroom has been relocated to the bedroom floor while the kitchen has been opened up to the main living area and is in the footprint of the old bathroom.

The idea of loft living is to take advantage of an open-plan layout of spaces as opposed to the conventional configuration of individual rooms. Previously this property was a live/work unit and that is why the rooms were more enclosed. Now completely residential, the entire space needed to be opened up and usable for day-to-day activities and to create a more sociable environment.

3 In the place of the old kitchen is now the dining area. With its double height volume it is flooded with light from the skylight above. A wall of storage adds visual impact. **4** A useful downstairs cloakroom has been placed in the original entrance to the old kitchen. This area combines storage and display, sometimes forgotten about in a practical room of this kind.

To enable heating pipework to get to opposite sides of the entire space and to get pipework to the central kitchen island and the downstairs cloakroom, the floor has been raised in the new kitchen, dining and hallway areas. This actually adds to the entire layout of the loft as it creates a slightly lower area for the main reception and den areas. It also allows for different floor surfaces, these in turn provide visually effective divisions of the space.

In the original entrance to the old kitchen, a small cloakroom has been installed. Using new technology for waste disposal, small diameter pipework could be used for this area. Within the old kitchen space, the new dining area is surrounded with floor-to-ceiling storage. Using chain store carcasses, the doors are simply painted MDF, cut to size as required, creating a visual and useful area. The central kitchen island is made from basic carcasses topped with a

white Corian work surface with set-in sink, with a dishwasher and washing machine housed beneath.

The all-white decoration blends in the old brick work with the new plaster work. A massive structural brick wall running the length of the space divides the area, keeping the location of certain elements such as kitchen and bathroom obvious due to the positions of openings and services.

In this kind of space, visual elements are an important and useful part of it. Due to the almost 50° vista, the grid of storage at one end relates well to the grid of the window the other end, bringing the two ends together.

EXTENDING YOUR SPACE

Searching for that perfect modern space can be a lengthy and often unrewarding undertaking. If you need more space or if you cannot find the right size of accommodation in the area in which you want to live, instead of going through the trauma of moving house, extending your space could prove the best alternative. Making your space bigger is becoming increasingly the way forward for adding a modern element to your existing or new space.

If you like where you live but are short of space, look at what you have and revalue all your options. You can go up, down or outwards. You can build on the roof, utilise the loft space, make use of the basement or cellar or add on to the rear or side elevation.

Of course all these options need careful consideration and lengthy conversations with the local planning officers and department. It is also a good idea to search for specialised firms in what you want before you get more involved in order to calculate if your ideas will come in within your budget.

Since these projects are usually mainly structural, the appropriate people need to be involved from the outset, to check that your proposals are feasible. Some developments do not require planning permission but most do need building permits and control.

First consider the potential of your roof space; with a typical pitched roof you can use the space inside the roof or extend out, or in some cases, raise the roof line. In a terrace of houses, if it is evident that some of the properties have roof extensions, it is usually a tell-tale sign that you can do the same. In conservation and protected areas, any extension will usually have to be in a similar style and built in similar materials to the surroundings. But in certain areas, some authorities are more forward thinking and allow totally modern additions. In an area of local development, you can sometimes be more adventurous with your scheme, using different materials and even include terraces and open rooftop spaces. Sometimes developing within the limits of the existing roof space can be limiting. An alternative option would be simply to use the roof space to increase the volume of the rooms beneath.

If your house has a flat roof or if you live on the top floor of an apartment block you may be able to build directly on top of your existing space. This can prove a lengthy and expensive project, but it can increase your apartment by 100 per cent. A glass box on the roof would be visually amazing, but you would need to consider the heat and insulation elements.

Your basement could be ripe for development, especially if the ceiling height is already adequate. Digging out deeper is possible and this favoured option will give you ample ceiling height; however, the whole space would need to be tanked out to stop the possibility of the water level encroaching the space. This basement space is usually ideal for accommodating a den or entertainment room, or for a kitchen-diner area, as it is away from the main part of the house and could be treated in a completely different decorative style to the main part of the home. If your house has a raised ground floor entry, the basement will usually have access to the garden level, giving important access between the indoor and outdoor space.

An addition is perhaps the easiest and least disruptive way of extending your space. If your garden is big enough you can extend quite far. With so many products available now for doors and windows, complete glass spaces can be built. If you are not overlooked these are ideal, but privacy is a factor to consider when planning the glass addition.

Of course the original spaces that are the openings to any new addition needs to blend in with the new. There needs to be a natural progression to the new space from the old.

1 The extension of glass panel constructiuon backs onto a 1930s Modernist house. The curves complement the bay window on the front elevation and the curved outhouses, now the kitchen, at the rear. **2** On the roof terrace of a riverside house the staircase opens up from the copper clad box. The outdoor kitchen saves running down three flights of stairs when using the area.

SIGNIFICANT IMPROVEMENTS

Extending your home is a way of getting more space where and when you want it, without the hassle of moving house.

In this house built by Don Chapell, the space has been enlarged more than once. Initially, this quite small house of 2800 sq ft was built by, and lived in, by the architect during his bachelor days. Once the present owners, Lois and Les Fishman, moved in, they realised the kitchen area was not going to be big enough for their two families combined. So they called in the original architect and cabinet maker, Dale Rieke, to expand the kitchen and eating areas. They pushed

1 The kitchen has been extended visibly by the slightly curving elevation above the car parking spaces. Behind is the raised roof line of the dining area. **2** Typical of Chapell's work, the kitchen colour scheme relates to the landscape seen through the windows. The irregularity of the cabinets is visually exciting.

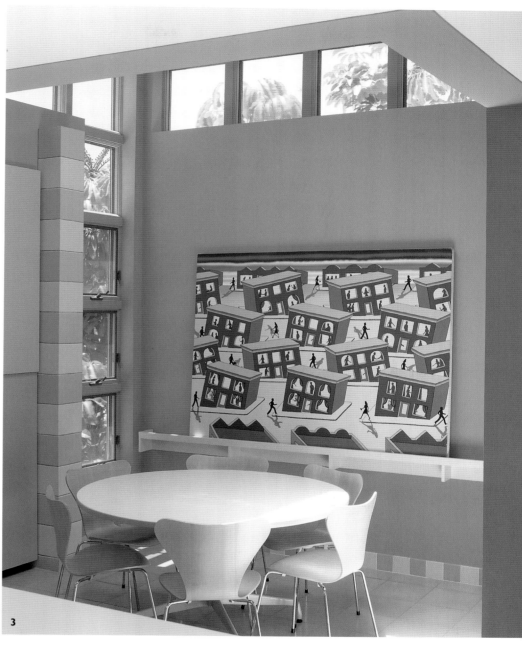

2

3

out the front elevation wall to a slight curve and raised the roof level to give greater volume to the dining area. When you are in the new kitchen you do not notice the curve of the new elevation, but it is apparent from the exterior. The cabinetry is signature Don Chapell, with the subtle colour selection relating to the tones and hues found in the surrounding landscape. The central island gives ample work surface for food preparation and entertaining.

The owners convinced Chapell to sell them the adjacent lot at the end of the quay, in order to ensure there was no possiblility of another house being built.

3 The new dining area has a raised roof which allows light to flood in through through its vertical and horizontal arrangement of windows. The painting inspired the colour scheme in this living area.

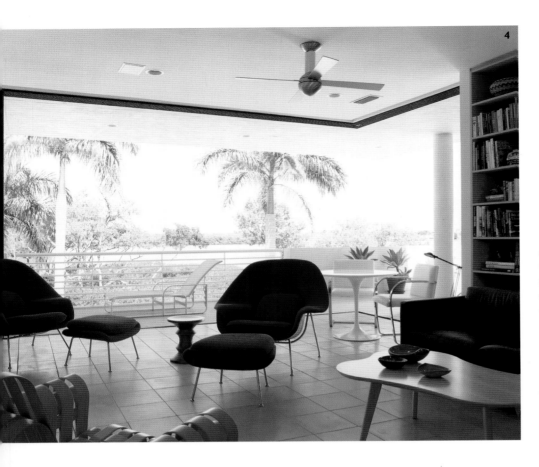

4 The corner glass doors that lead onto the terrace slide into pockets when open, allowing for a complete inside-outside lifestyle. The purple womb chair brings in the landscape beyond. **5** The existing sitting room has an opening to allow views of the new sitting room beyond. This divides the areas but entices you to experience the new space.

The Fishmans had planned for Chapell to extend the house and add a wing to it. But due to his premature death they called in Guy Peterson. A follower of work by Paul Rudolph, as was Chapell, Peterson seemed the best candidate.

This new wing was to almost double the volume of the existing house. Peterson suggested removing the side wall of the house, not to give access, but to open up the visual aspect of the new living room beyond. The Fishmans were not sure about this, but they soon realised it was 'one of the most signficant improvements to their living space'.

The existing living space, with built-in furniture by Lois's son Bill Mostow, also includes classics of the 20th century. In the new living area more classics tie this area to the existing space. Wilson Stiles, responsible for the interior design, has

AFTER ABOVE
The new wing includes a new sitting room with bedrooms and shower room for the family. Part of the wall of the existing house has been removed to give a new vista from the old to the new. The shape of the new wing relates to the overall form of the plot.

used colour from the landscape to successfully bring the outside in, as in Chapell's kitchen design. The Saarinen womb chair matches the bougainvilea nearby.

At the far end of the house, a projecting triangular wing outlines the position of the new shower room. This angled space relates to the overall plot shape and brings the house to a halt. Light pouring in from the vertical floor-to-ceiling slit window gives a feeling of infinity, and links the coloured mosiac tiled walls to the natural seascape outside.

As Les Fishman says, 'we have bright vistas from room to room and every room has a view'.

6 The triangular projection at the end of the house relates to the shape of the plot following the coastal line. Within the tapered walls a large shower room is housed. **7** Fitted cabinetry is angled to fit the irregular space of this area. **8** The tile used in the shower area relates to the landscape outside.

ROOFTOP LIVING

This former warehouse

building has been carefully converted into a chic and spacious residential loft.

Having lived in Tribeca, Manhattan, for many years, the owners of this space joined forces with their neighbours to try to find a building to convert for themselves. They found a six-storey building that was built just after the turn of the 20th century in the early 1900s. It still retained many of the typical loft features, such as the bare brick walls and huge wooden rafters. Between them, they calculated they would share the top two floors, that is the 5th and 6th.

Working with architect firm The Downtown Group, they called in Mark Winkelman to work out the division of space. After various considerations they decided to divide the two floors with a diagonal wall, giving a wedge-shaped unit that is about 60ft at one end and 50ft at the other. Working on the plans was a bit of a problem. The wedge-shaped plan creates a long widening entry to the space. To get the best south-facing views, the architects came up with the design for a new floor on top of the existing building. So the basic ideas for the space were decided. The main living room would be in the new roof top extension which would overlook the entrance hall. This meant the kitchen, dining area, study and master

I From the roof terrace the roof line is more apparent. The wall on the left is the dividing line between the two lofts. To the right is the cut out for the courtyard below. **2** Above the staircase, the roof lights bring light right down to the children's level on the lower floor. These thin metal beams appear to be keeping the roof under control. **3** From the new roof top floor, the cedar clad hyper parabolic roof sweeps across the living area. The wall of glass doors opens onto the large roof terrace.

3

AFTER RIGHT
The new roof extension with its hyper parabolic ceiling line tops the already split-floor loft. Its winglike span hovers above the existing beams of the old building.

bedroom and bathrooom would be on the 6th floor, the entry floor. The children would have their own space down on the fifth floor. There would also be an open courtyard garden on the main floor, with three sides opening.

Using a computer moderl, Winkelman and Valledor, the project designers, were able to work out the precise angles for the new roof line. A cedar clad hyper parabolic ceiling and roof was designed. This roof line would sweep up like a wing above the existing heavy beams of the old building.

The steel staircase sweeps up from the entrance area, under the wooden supports of the 6th floor, and is naturally lit from above by the glazed panels that run along the edge of the roof at the dividing diagonal wall.

Throughout the entire loft, well designed cherry wood fitted storage and kitchen cabinets have been installed. With the study leading off from the kitchen and into the courtyard, this space also becomes an informal breakfast area when necessary.

At the roof level, an entire wall of metal framed doors and windows can be opened for access to the huge roof terrace. With a cut out for the courtyard garden down below, this outdoor space works well for entertaining.

When working on a project of this scale, architects and engineers have to be consulted. With so many flat roofs around you can imagine this could be the best way to increase the size of your home without moving house.

INTERIOR EXTENSION

Converting space that is already part of the house, but not included in the liveable areas, is often overlooked. These days having a garage is a luxury, but with many older properties, a standard garages is just not big enough for today's average-size car or 4 x 4 vehicle. Whether it is part of the main structure or an original addition to the side, these integral spaces are ideal extensions to the existing living space.

In this house, built in 1935, the integral garage is only just under 8ft wide, and with the doors open, the opening narrows to just over 7ft wide. Garages today are more for storage it seems: the more space you have, the more you need.

Luckily, with this house, the decision to develop the garage space was decided while the whole house was being worked on.

Originally, this house had no access to the large back garden besides a regular back door from the kitchen. Even the rooms upstairs did not have access to the flat roof at the rear. Strangely, there are two balconies with doors opening onto them at the front of the house, overlooking the road. However, with well-positioned trees and more planting, these are now more private.

While bricked-up openings were cut out of the end wall of the garage, the back wall of the room above was removed

1 Looking out from the new summer room through the sliding doors, you can enjoy a great view of the swimming pool. This room, for relaxing and summer eating, looks like it has always been part of the house, even though it was originally the garage then converted to its current use. Even in the winter with the doors closed it is still a great space to use. The dropped ceiling has been painted to complement the pool and exaggerate the blue skies of summer. **2** The back elevation of the house shows how the bacony and large space beyond the old garage give space for lounging and access to the pool. The door and railings above look like that they have always been there.

BEFORE ABOVE
The cramped entrance hall and warren of small rooms around the kitchen area make the ground floor very traditional compared to the very modern exterior. The original garage space takes up a great deal of the floor plan, ideal to convert.

AFTER ABOVE
The garage doors have been replaced with a solid wall. The partition walls have been removed, giving an open plan approach to the kitchen and entrance hall. Double doors open on to the back garden.

3 The two porthole windows are inserted into the wall that was originally the entrance to the garage. Luckily these were salvaged from other areas within the house. The dining set is by Aalto **4** From the original living room you can see into the new summer room and out of the French doors where the kitchen was originally located. The central staircase has been stripped of layers of paint to carry on the wood flooring up to the next level. **5** The downstairs cloakroom had to be made slightly smaller to allow for an opening to the new room. The circular window theme carries through.

to accommodate French doors which let in great views of the garden and the sea beyond. An opening from the hallway was made to the old garage and to enable this, the large cloakroom under the staircase had to be shortened. You can now look from the existing living room into the new summer room.

Large sliding doors, similar to those used in car showrooms, were installed on the ground level at the end of the garage, so that almost all of it could be open during summer months. In the room above, Crittall metal-framed French doors were installed, to match the existing windows used throughout the existing house, and a tubular nautical railing fitted around the balcony area, to match those at the front of the house.

The old garage had two porthole windows on the side which add to the overall nautical theme. Inside the new room, reclaimed wood block flooring was sourced and laid with a staggered joint to match the kitchen area. Two more porthole windows were installed in the wall that

replaced the double doors. The theme from other parts of the house is carried on throughout, using mainly furniture by Alvar Aalto.

Elsewhere in the house the ground floor was opened up. There was originally a warren of rooms in the central core of the house. A large walk-in coat cupboard, the kitchen, a WC and the maid's room were all removed to make an open-plan space to house the new kitchen. French doors, the same as those in the room above the garage, were installed into the same position as the original kitchen window, opening up this area to the back garden as well. In all the ground floor rooms with openings, the inside and outside flooring materials have been laid as near to the same levels as possibles to create an uninterrupted plane.

This extension of space shows how important it is to retain features and specifications from the existing house and structure. To use new versions of the windows but keeping to the original proportions is one of the most important elements when working on an older building.

This apartment has been extended by taking over the space laterally in the adjoining building. The original small studio apartment on the upper west side of Manhattan, with studio and kitchen on one floor and a bedroom and bathroom on the upper floor, was developed two years previously. Being a total renovation, new materials were used, both natural and synthetic. Refurbished vintage steel cabinets have been used in the kitchen alongside the natural olive wood used for the new cabinets and shelving. Concrete has been used for the countertops with blackened steel used for the fireplace.

The chance to extend laterally is unusual. In this case, as the two townhouses are in fact part of the same Coop ownership, they were seen as one property in the eyes of the Department of Building. It helped enormously that the floor levels were the same.

In the adjacent townhouse, there is a sitting room, bathroom, bedroom and a small office area. In this area, more synthetic materials have been used. In the bathroom, there is a resin and pebble slab floor and there are fibreglass sliding panels to open up and close off certain areas.

The apartment now has two bathrooms. The original one on the top floor is more traditional in approach with mosaic tile and stone floor, while the new bathroom has a more up-to-date approach. This space is treated as an open shower room with a slot in the floor for drainage.

The total decoration of the apartment, with a mix of vintage and oriental objects and furnishings, has a calming and timeless ambience. The use of colour, texture and materials has created an eclectic mix of style and culture. From the Bertoia breakfast stools to the railway trolley car used as a table, each individual item works well with the next. Both renovations are by Ogawa Depardon and are united by a roof terrace, accessed from either unit via custom-made pivoting doors.

In this kind of extension, taking over the space next to you is an ambitious way to gain more accommodation. It is perhaps an extravagant way to extend, but in a way it is somewhat similar to converting your basement or roofspace. Initially you will end up with two of this and two of that, but it will increase you living space to at least double its size without having to sell up and move.

AFTER RIGHT
What was once a duplex on one side and a railroad apartment on the other have been united creating a double reception, study area and more private sitting room at the front of the buildings. Outside, the roof terrace becomes and outside room.

1 This is the kitchen in the original studio apartment with bathroom and bedroom upstairs. Refurbished steel cabinets have been used in this zone. The Stained oak staircase wraps around the kitchen and continues the dark floor upstairs. **2** From the second phase renovation you can see the original studio. This space in the adjoining townhouse has a bleached oak floor while the original apartment has a black ink-stained finish.

GLAZED LEVELS UNITED

On entering this five-storey Victorian

townhouse in Brooklyn, New York, you have no idea what you will find at the back of the house. The front elevation retains all of its original features, doors, windows and ironwork, but once the front door is opened you realise that there is too much light filtering through the engraved glass doors for this to be an entirely original house. What would have been a dark passage to the original kitchen is now a floodlit entrance to a double height atrium, housing the kitchen on the first floor and the dining area below. The New York based firm Ogawa Depardon has added one of its modern signature pieces to an otherwise aged and traditional home. This two-storey addition has united the former maze of tiny rooms on the lower floor with the space on the entrance level.

Through what must have been the french doors out of the main reception room onto a terrace is now the new kitchen. With a typical Ogawa Depardon ceiling hung unit dividing the space, the kitchen is open to the room below and contains veiws of the garden beyond. The new staircase flows naturally down to the new entertaining floor that houses the dining room and offers one large den space that can be divided by sliding the glass partitions. Leaving these partition doors open enables the use of the entire lower level, making it a focal area for socialising.

BEFORE LEFT
The original layout of the lower level was a series of very dark rooms. This lower level of the house was a self-contained unit that housed its own kitchen and bathroom.

AFTER BELOW LEFT
Now the entire lower level has been opened up to house a shower room and wet bar and these now replace the previous areas. The removal of the rear and dividing walls has managed to visually create more space.

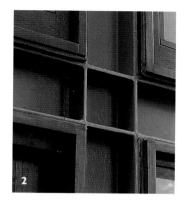

1 The double height extension on the rear of this Victorian house replaces a smaller lower level box room and opens up the living areas of the house. The sliding doors bring the outside in and, while modern in construction, still retain the three-window grid of the original house elevation. 2 An aesthetically pleasing steel frame creates the grid for the new windows. The thinness of the edge of the steel beams gives a lightness to the overall mass. 3 The dining area at the lower level opens onto the garden. The stairway from the kitchen above sweeps down into the space. The interior, created by Michael Formica, brings colour into an area that could easily be dull and dark.

BEFORE ABOVE TOP
The rear of the house was originally a mish mash of windows and doors with a small rear addition and an outside staircase. There did already exist a terrace from the 2nd floor rooms.

AFTER ABOVE BELOW
The new addition echoes the three window grid of the floors above and dramatically increase the amount of light that floods the lower floors.

4 In the kitchen, the bank of cabinets houses the dishwasher and the sink. To work here and look over the level below and through into the garden could not be any better. From this level the stairs lead directly to the dining area, forming a natural flow from the one level to another. **5** From what must have once been the original opening at the back of the house, we look into the new kitchen space. The ceiling-hung storage unit divides the space and balances the grid of the windows beyond. The matching floor from the old to the new unites the space — an important element often overlooked when extending your space.

In some ways when we do this kind of addition that houses the kitchen and dining area we are tempted to put the kitchen down into the lowest part of the house. By placing this kitchen where it is on the entrance level, it is more usable and accessible from the bedroom and children's floors above.

It also means that the entire lower floor can be given over to a general family room, thus keeping the main salon type room off the entrance hall as a quiet and calm space and retaining the original layout.

From the garden the elevation of the new additions follows the original three-window grid of the rear of the house. It has a very simple cross frame skeleton that carries the glazed units, both fixed and opening. The mix of steel and timber frames mellows the whole appearance and gives the feeling that it has been there a while, so that it naturally gels into the surroundings.

Overall the addition to the house has been created for the whole family to use and enjoy. With the extension, the house is now flexible and opens up otherwise useless spaces that one often finds in older homes like this.

BEFORE RIGHT ABOVE
The lower level before was basically two rooms with a kitchen and bathroom in a separate unit to the main house.

AFTER RIGHT BELOW
With the introduction of a staircase from the new kitchen, the lower level is now incorporated into the entire space of the house.

THE HOME DISSECTED

Page 92 Contrasting floor surfaces give a distinctive division to an open-plan space, at the same time adding textural contrast and clean visual lines.

I Highlighting the original structural elements of this Amsterdam house gives uniformity and proportion to a modern home. **2** Again in Amsterdam, this wall of storage is divided up into smaller units marked by flat-fronted doors in various sizes. While being useful it is also visually exciting. The chair is by Arne Jacobsen.

Whether you have just bought a new home, flat or industrial unit, or maybe you have decided that now is the time to update your existing space, where to start and what to do are the two main questions. This chapter breaks down the elements of the home and gives solutions to inspire you.

Going through the various degrees of modernisation, there are certain aspects that relate to all of them. But perhaps there are just some elements that you want to update. When making your home more modern you may decide just to work on the storage areas or just your floors. You do not have to do it all. Selecting what is for you, you can work out what level you are aiming for and you can get some idea of what approach to take and what to do first.

Before you even consider the elements, try to work out what you want to achieve. Assess your personal requirements, those of your children if you have them, whether you work from home and also that you will, of course, be entertaining your friends. Getting the works done in the correct order is one of the most important parts of the whole procedure.

If you are taking the decorative modernisation route you will be looking to install new flooring materials, wall coverings and paints and maybe new or updated furniture. Of course you will not be installing anything as major as new timber floors, but you could try some of the new easy-to-lay flooring panels. You could paint your floorboards or you could simply lay new carpets. On the walls you can paint, paper or apply some other finish appropriate to the situation.

2

I would say, for the most impact, new furniture pieces for relaxing, storage and display will change the home drastically. You can be more organised, show off your treasured items and be able to put your feet up when all the work is done.

Updating more substantial features in the home will include laying more permanent new or reclaimed timber floors, ceramic-tile floors or any other types that are fixed. You may want to change doors to rooms, wardrobes and cupboards. In the kitchen you might update your existing cabinets with more modern and sleek doors. You may want to build in more unit furniture for display and storage and you may make a new focal point in the main reception area by updating the fireplace. Elsewhere you could replace the entire staircase –

3 In the lobby of this Sarasota, Florida, home a custom-built unit shows off a collection of European and Scandinavian ceramics. **4** These shelves designed by Alvar Aalto in the 1930s are still so modern. A combination of found objects and art are put together in harmony. **5** A contrast of flooring materials here defines the spaces within the home, with terrazzo in the shower room, cork in the kitchen and oak boards in the hallway. The threshold strip is made of stainless steel.

6 Behind the zig-zag staircase is a series of storage areas with doors of polycarbonate, giving a translucency to these areas. **7** A wall of walnut veneered doors runs the length of the house. Behind is ample storage for clothing.

this is perhaps a little adventurous, but it will be a dramatic change. Of course furniture, furnishings and lighting will all play a part in updating your home. New hanging light fixtures and perhaps recessed spots can create great effects within the home without too much disruption.

If you are to reorganise your space, there are so many more elements to consider. Maybe you will only be working on the main reception and kitchen areas, but that is enough. Think about uniting the space with completely new flooring throughout. In a bedroom and bathroom area try using a duo storage wall that would divide these two zones. Plan a lighting scheme that is flexible for many areas and uses — one that is dimmable and low energy, for example. Reorganising your space gives you a chance to get your whole life sorted out, as you can include ample storage and that all-important work space.

If you are considering extending your home, every element will need to be considered. If you are going into the roof space, for instance, you will need a new staircase. In other extended or added-on areas you will need to unite the old with the new by using the same or similar flooring throughout. You will need lighting, you will need storage and display elements and you may have a chance to include a new focal point to the extra space. If you are adding onto the back or side of the house you will need to select windows and doors as well.

Whatever type of modernisation you go for, lighting and furniture are the key visual elements. The lighting has to illuminate the room when necessary and also create atmosphere and ambience. The furniture has to be comfortable and do its job, but it also has to look good as it will dictate the feel of the space. Use either new design, vintage or reproduction classics or thrift-shop finds — it is all up to you — but they must work together to create the ideal modern home.

A good floor can make or
break a great interior. Whether you have
floorboards, either painted, sanded or
polished, for example, hardwood strips,
plywood panels, concrete, tile or rubber,
the choice is seemingly endless.

Working with what you already have
is the best way to start. With good old
basic pine floorboards you can sand
and polish them, stain them, paint them
or you can use them as a sound solid
surface for applying a multitude of
other floor treatments. As long as it
is well secured and pretty level, the
timber floor can be a background
material for many more decorative
materials, especially other timbers and
various sheet floorings, such as birch
plywood tongue-and-groove panels or
more unusual finishes such as bamboo.

1 On the staircase and landing an oak plank floor shows the irregularity of the area. The walls appear to float as the flooring carries on beneath. **2** This plank floor runs throughout the apartment. Beyond these sliding panels is a Woodnotes rug that defines this space, a bedroom. **3** This floor is a good example of using a semi-gloss sealer to preserve the wood's natural appearance. **4** This painted wood-strip floor shows how easy it is to update an otherwise tired and worn-out one. **5** Birch-faced plywood tongue-and-groove panels slot together to make an instant new floor. This flooring from Finland now comes pre-finished, to make it even easier to install.

6 Using the same material for the treads of a staircase and for the landing areas maintains the flow. Here laminated walnut slabs are oiled for their protection.
7 A combination of the dark wood and the lighter limestone works in this totally new interior. the softness of the wood does seem to balance with the hardness of the stone.

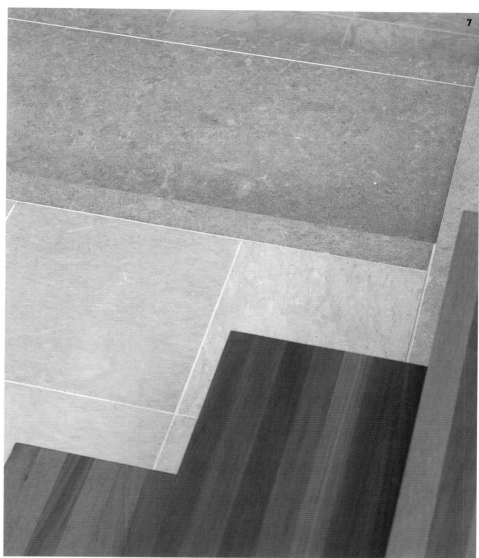

These days it seems easier and more instant to lay a new pre-finished floor over what you already have. But a good well-finished wide-boarded floor has a certain feeling of 'I'm here for eternity'. It does give soul to a space and will warm up many a sterile stark interior. The white-painted floorboard gives a feeling of a country or seaside interior. The black-painted floorboard gives a slicker, more city feel and creates a hard-edged crisp living space.

In open-plan spaces, which are being used more and more these days, the use of various flooring materials on one level is a way of defining the space for certain uses. A timber surface can be used in the living and sleeping areas and a tile or stone surface in the kitchen and wet areas – common sense dictates the appropriate product.

With the conversion of more and more industrial buildings the re-use of existing flooring is well accepted. The old flagstones of a barn, the concrete floor, polished or painted, or the installation of a poured rubber floor, usually found in operating theatres, are becoming common options for the home.

The material, the colour, the price and the availability all add to the effectiveness of a new floor. If you can lay or install a new floor yourself it can be a pretty immediate project. If you want something a little more special, calling in the experts can be the only way.

A terrazzo floor covering a complete space gives a cool and calm united space. While it is a lengthy and costly experience it is well worth the time and money.

It is amazing how so much good flooring has been covered up over the years. Whether it be wide Georgian oak boards, 1930s herringbone pine parquet or Victorian encaustic tile, to restore and keep what you have, to replace it with a

8 Brick flooring laid in an alternate grid fashion gives a sense of space and proportion to this kitchen floor. **9** In a former industrial building the shabby concrete floors were updated with a coat of floor paint. The colour was matched to newly laid concrete screed to resemble the original floor.

10 Limestone squares run throughout the entire ground level of this house. It acts as a great background for mid-20th-century modern furniture. **11** Clear or pigmented epoxy binders can be fused wtih multi-coloured or natural stone; this one is marble and resin. Many such floors are fast-curing and unaffected by sunlight, which makes them popular for outdoor use too. **12** Poured terrazzo floors used from around 1930 to 1960 are often found under newer floor coverings. Luckily it can be easily restored, re-polished and filled if necessary. Terrazzo is often used for worktops and is now becoming a popular alternative for a new floor.

13 Here the use of a natural Berber carpet complements the stacked brick feature of the chimney rising from the floor below. It also balances with the grid of the Bertoia chair. **14** On a concrete floor a new runner has been placed. Besides making the floor kinder to the feet it leads the eye into the gallery area of this apartment. **15** The colour of this carpet was selected to tie in with the landscape, to bring the outside in. **16** This new carpet is silk with metal thread detail, a fresh take on a traditional carpet method, bringing it up to date. It also introduces some pattern to an otherwise unadorned interior.

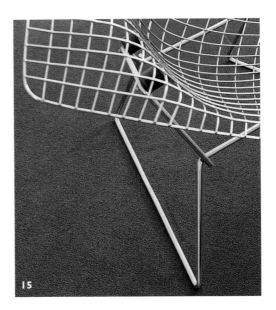

newer version or to completely change the floor surface is entirely up to you. After all, the floor of your home takes up a vast surface area of your space. It has to be comfortable to use, good to look at and work in the area it is allocated to.

The use of flooring to define the space within is a good and less disruptive way of making a home more modern. To use a mix of carpet, timber and ceramic flooring in one space will create an interesting and comfortably united space.

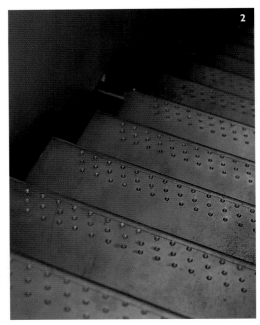

1 In this Tribeca loft in New York the staircase follows the diagonal partition wall with the neighbouring unit. It cuts through the original roof line and enters into the new room. 2 The steel treads have been drilled with circular recesses to act as anti-slip devices. Here you can see the simple steel fixings to the wall. 3 When you enter the loft the staircase leads your eye to the upper level, but with the void below you also note that it descends to the lower quarters. The mix of steel for the upper treads and timber for the lower relates to the construction of the original building.

Below stairs in years past was where your staff of servants carried out their duties. Below stairs today could mean storage, home office, utility room or even a downstairs cloakroom. The staircase now is not just a facility for getting from one floor to another – it can also be a decorative item of visual effect for the modern home and it can act as a valuable area of dual use. It will take you up and down the stairs but can also be your place of work.

As a means of getting from one level of the home to another, the staircase can be straight, spiral, in a recess, in the centre of the room or hidden in an enclosed hallway. The proportions must be correct, and the safety aspects must be looked into. There are certain constraints regarding the riser and tread dimensions that must be taken into consideration. But when it comes to the visual importance of the staircase it is the materials that can make it stand out from the rest.

Nowadays, the staircase is a feature that many people will consider altering, and whether to relocate it entirely or just to re-finish it are just two of the options. With open-plan types of accommodation being increasingly popular, the fact that the staircase is more visual element has given it a more important role in the modernisation of the home.

3

4 Rising up against a rustic stone wall, a simple modern staircase made from steel 'I'-profile beams has had fixings added for the treads. The handrail was applied once in situ. **5** The typical Victorian staircase has been updated here with coloured paint and polished treads. The ornateness of the bannisters gives a sense of the past to the interior.

The use of glass as a contemporary structural element as well as a visual component has helped to increase its use for staircase construction. With glass treads, balustrades and landings a glass staircase can look stunning and bring much-needed light to an otherwise dark hallway.

The use of steel as a staircase frame has also helped so much with creating the modern staircase. With treads of metal, plywood or any type of timber a metal-framed spiral stairway can look timeless in a classic setting. With many alternatives available off the shelf the metal staircase offers an almost instant transformation. With the help of a welder any shape or proportion of construction can be created, thus making it unique to the space in which it is installed.

When it comes to the banister and balustrades, the choice of whether to enclose or leave open is yours. A solid side to a staircase can give a valuable wall space and also create storage space beneath. The open tread gives a feel of openness, especially if the staircase is within an open space.

In my experience, the relocation of a staircase can make the most drastic modernisation to any home. In an older house the basic staircase can take up so much room that to re-configure it and maybe move it can open up the space in a whole new way. Turning a staircase can give a larger, more welcome entrance hall with less need of a turn or a half landing and the modern elements in its construction inevitably make the whole place feel more modern.

6 A spiral staircase rises up from the main living room to the upper bedroom level. A spiral, while taking up less floor space than a traditional staircase, can dominate a space, but it does allow the eye to see through it. 7 This built-in staircase follows the line of the circular room. Its monolithic construction makes it both a visual feature and a structural one. The treads are made of slate. 8 This staircase divides into two, one side going to the bedroom area and the other leading to the outside terrace. Constructed from simple off-the-shelf elements, it has been customised with a solid bannister one side and tension wires the other. The open side allows light to penetrate through to the level below. 9 An oak staircase made from simple slabs without any moulding or detail appears to float between the two white-painted walls. There is a gap either side that accentuates this illusion. A tubular stainless-steel hand rail helps you climb the three-storey staircase.

1 In this Los Angeles home, a mid-century classic, the full-height sliders open up the indoor room to the outside, creating that important indoor/outdoor lifestyle.

Natural light is a valuable element of the workings of the space within the modern home. The style of the windows in the home are inevitably inherited with the building you buy. In a house, the front elevation is usually within a terrace or a row of other houses, and in my opinion there is nothing worse than one house on the street that has had its elevation altered with wrongly proportion windows inserted. It is always best to keep to the originals if you can on the public face of a building.

The back elevation is a different story though. Here, you could change every opening to create larger windows, to create a different format of windows or to make the whole back of the house into one big window. Getting the balance right is the clever part. The best way to do it is to consider the windows if and when you add on an extension, to tie the old in with the new. This would be a natural progression to modernisation. With so many types of construction and materials you can get a good match to the originals or a good complementary

3 High-level strip windows are great for areas in which you want privacy, especially when you live in a built-up area. They bring light in without the worry about being overlooked. In this house in Sarasota, Florida, the clerestory window runs the length of the living area along the street side of the house. **4** An original feature such as this six-sided window gives character and soul to this renovated space. Retaining elements such as this keeps you in touch with the origins of the building. **5** This curved wall of window features custom-built bent sections of glass. Built in the 1930s, this bay was included to capture the distant views of the sea beyond and the surrounding landscape. The window ledge is poured terrazzo. **6** In what was once the out-building to a 1930s house in Frinton-on-Sea, Essex, an oval curved window reflects the curves of the building, as does the circular skylight.

style. In some ways it is best to stick to the same materials, but perhaps to change the format. There is a huge variety in the style of window that has been available throughout recent history, from the timber sashes of the 19th century to the metal frames of the 1930s and 1950s and the plastic windows of the late 20th century. Even the UPVC windows being used everywhere these days can look great if used in the right place and with the right proportions within the elevations.

7 In an addition to a Victorian school building, this modern wall of glass is softened with Venetian blinds. This area opens up onto a courtyard garden. **8** Light from this hallway is let into an internal room via this high-level strip of window. **9** In a room that is overlooked, a small grid pattern helps distort images. The up-rising blind ensures total privacy. The grid of windows is an original feature of this mews house. **10** This full-height panel of glass allows necessary light through to an otherwise dark stair well.

DOORS

1 The original front door of this San Francisco townhouse provides an immediate understanding of the house you are about to enter. It completes the Victorian façade and the modern pieces placed nearby show how effective mixing styles can be. **2** Pivoting doors provide a wider opening. This entrance door has a woven steel insert. In this lobby, the front wall is entirely glazed with various openings. The lower-level window acts as a ventilator, capturing the cross breeze. **3** In the same house as above, the walkway to the upper levels has a wall of windows that have louvred screens, which work as sunshades as well as privacy panels. This gives a certain serene atmosphere to the whole space.

When it comes to doors,

the use of an original style door on the front elevation is always a good start. But when you get inside, the internal doors can be whatever you want. You can have conventional hinged doors, sliding doors, folding ones or those that roll into a pocket at one side of the opening. Door frames can be removed or adjusted to give floor-to-ceiling openings or relocated to open different aspects of the rooms in question. They may even be used to unite or divide two or more areas.

The materials are so varied that there is no reason for using the wrong door. Glass or glazed internal doors will bring essential light to dark areas and gloomy corridors, and to create a more naturally flowing link between each room.

In a more open-plan arrangement, sliding doors can give the appearance of a lot more space. The slider that goes into

4 In a Tim Seibert house built in the 1960s in Sarasota, Florida, this area within the house has sliding timber doors that enable this space to be either enclosed for privacy or opened up for entertaining. These panels slide into pockets so that they can be completely concealed. **5** The top floor houses the bedrooms and main bathroom. The master bedroom spreads across the back of the house. The use of a sliding panel as a door unites the spaces when open without taking up valuable room. When it is closed it looks like a seamless part of the wall. **6** This Amsterdam residence has many sliding doors and panels, facilitating a totally flexible space that can be adapted for many uses. These deep red panels run along the first-floor landing.

7 These aluminium-framed glass doors run along a track carved into the stone floor. Keeping a uniformity throughout the areas both sides of the track also retains an uninterrupted floor when the doors are opened. **8** Three glazed panels make up the entire screen wall to this area. The dining area can be completely exposed or cut off from the kitchen, ideal for entertaining when a more intimate atmosphere is required. A single fixed glass panel runs along the staircase area.

a pocket is even more space conscious – while the wall taking the door needs to be thicker, to provide enough of a recess, the actual wall either side of the door will remain clear for other uses.

The door is an important part of the modern interior. While to some it is a great idea to have no doors, just openings, the flexibility of being able to open up and close off a room or area does make the overall space feel larger.

On the whole, the windows and the doors of your modern space should complement the architecture and materials of the original building, but they must also do the job required of them – to bring in light, to ventilate where necessary and to divide or unite the areas within the home.

8

WALLS AND WALL TREATMENTS

For me it's the walls within the space that make it a home. I've been in many homes where the owners have instantly removed every wall so that now they are living in a barn-like space with the furniture pushed against the exterior walls and pointless groupings dotted around. With open-plan living so often being one step forward towards modernisation, the balance of which wall is removed, which wall is left and which wall is installed is so important.

In my loft space, I am fortunate enough to have a very thick structural wall that runs the length of, and divides, the entire space. This gives a natural break-up of the space. Compared with my neighbour's unit, which has no division, it feels twice the size. This is because my neighbour's unit is completely open – there are no hidden or surprise areas. What you see is what you get.

The placing of walls is very important. Whether they are solid, sliding, floor to ceiling or at low level, they are there to define the space and the use of the area within. The sliding wall, of course, creates the most flexible space. To be able to open up or enclose particular areas of a home with moveable screens, either solid or opaque, keeps the entire space usable. A space with no dividing walls gives less scope to place furniture, artwork and entertainment equipment.

1 In an industrial building, now a home, the original brick walls have been painted to bring them up to date. Layer upon layer of paint has been applied to achieve a uniform even finish. **2** The concrete block wall, forming a large-scale grid pattern, makes a great backdrop to contemporary furniture and furnishings. Here it has been painted dark red to create a dramatic interior.

3 Paint techniques have been used to create a false cornice. The wall blends into the ceiling and the highlighted line gives depth between the planes.

4 The fireplace wall divides this house, with the kitchen on one side and the living area on the other. The use of colour exaggerates this division. **5** The subtle finish to this wall unites the painting and the staircase. It is pale grey with a pearlised effect. **6** Retaining the 1970s bronze-finish ceramic tiles works well in this contemporary bathroom. They complement the heavy timber beams reflected in the mirror inserted into the grid at the appropriate height above the sink.

When taking on a shell space it can be quite difficult to decide what to do. The best way to start is to break down the space according to how you want to use each area. Also decide how flexible you want each space to be and work out whether the walls should be solid, glass, moveable or fixed – these decisions are all part of the total initial concept. A series of walls can create visual space and make your everyday functions at home work for you from the start.

The treatments used on walls can make them stand out as features or disappear so that they are simply a division of space. Deciding what to use on the wall surface is always a difficult task. If you paint: what colour, what finish, where to stop

7

8

7 In this Finnish apartment by Ulla Koskinen an opaque glass wall allows, in the daytime, light from the living room to flow into the bathroom, while it acts as a full-length illumination at night. **8** These industrial pre-formed glass panels are set in a curve in this extension. They give a distorted view, which diffuses the outside, whatever the weather. **9** On the top floor of a San Francisco town house a bathroom with a glass roof is concealed behind this wall of glass. So strong is the midday sun that it almost appears to be flood lit.

10 In this bathroom, light floods through the full-height opaque glass wall. **11** With all traces of plaster removed, the old brick walls in this Victorian house add character, texture and pattern. **12** A selection of colour tiles laid in a random pattern gives a great sense of disorder to this well-planned bathroom. Tiled floor to ceiling, it is both practical and unusually exciting. **13** The concrete block wall in this Gene Leedy-designed home runs from the outside in. A brick floor has been laid in the same fashion to complement it.

and start the colour? If you wallpaper: what style, where to use it? If you clad, what should you use: wood, textured panels, glass, plexiglass or even metal? Any application to a wall must be done for the right reason.

The use of colour on the right wall is a task in itself. To paint every wall white can look great but it is an easy option. The highlighting of different adjacent walls can add further dimensions and give illusions of space in many interiors. Oliver Hill, an architect and designer working in the 1930s, would use various pastel colours on walls that would balance and complement the light coming into the room.

Experience the spaces before you apply any decoration. You can see where the light falls and reflects so you can try out colours to get the best results. Even the use of various tones of one colour can add dimension and space to a room.

FOCAL POINTS

A room with a view does make sense, even if the view is contained within the room. The focal point – the fireplace, for example – gives a focus to the room. It is somewhere to start from. Okay, not every room has a fireplace, but in the main living area it usually does exist so the fireplace is the obvious focus. What should you do to make it more modern and update your interior?

It's good to have this type of focal point, but the traditional Victorian surround can be somewhat sad in a modern interior. A good simple marble fireplace is timeless and would give a classic modern feel to any room. With the

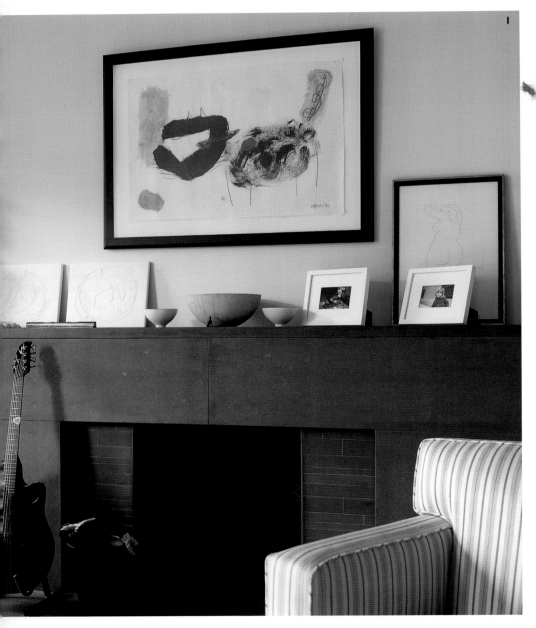

1 In New York this wide fireplace of steel and stone is a heavy welcoming sight when you enter this room. 2 A simple wood-burning stove has been concealed behind a stainless-steel sheath to enhance its appearance and to create a focal point in the open-plan space it which it stands. 3 This massive chimney breast dominates this space yet works as a visual screen to the entrance area of this house, affording privacy when necessary.

use of different fuels the fireplace can now be easily installed even without a chimney. The hole-in-the-wall style fireplace has become popular recently. Referring to the 1970s for its look, the high level slot can easily be used for other purposes besides heating. And with more ready-made surrounds now available there is one for most styles and budgets.

Today we often see the plasma screen as a focal point in the room. This is so much better than the television set that until recently was often the central attraction in the main living room. With the use of this type of entertainment equipment viewing at least it is quite discreet and is really now treated as a decorative element to the interior.

Bookcases or display units can also be focal points. An alcove can house an instant installation especially created for your collection of historic pots to form a focal experience. A focal point could also be a great painting or a sculpture on a plinth, for example. This is what draws the eye into the room and gives an ambience to the whole space.

5

4 The plasma screen, the new focal point in today's home, has been set into this three-quarters-high wall. The home now has a new necessity. **5** The long low recessed shelf functions as a focus in the same way a fireplace would. It is also good for display, and it would give an instant atmosphere to any space.

I On the landing and above the staircase of this modernist house rows of low-voltage spots lights have been installed parallel to and close to the wall edge, thus bringing light to the rising staircase and the artwork. **2** Recessed group lighting that is flush with the ceiling creates a neat and tidy alternative to the individual downlighter.

How important lighting is cannot be overlooked. There is nothing worse than a dimly lit room with inadequate lighting facilities. Whether you are using uplit, downlit, concealed, central, floor, wall or occasional lighting, or ideally a clever combination of some or all of these, you can light up your interior in any way you want.

If you are doing major refurbishment work on your home the introduction of downlighters or built-in lighting is a good option as all the work of recessing unsightly wires can be done while the ceilings are down and the floors are up.

The most important principle of lighting is the use of the right type of illumination for the task in question. There are basically two types of lighting, the directional type and that which is purely decorative. It then breaks down further into recessed, surface mounted, concealed or free-standing styles.

With the recessed method there are endless options for low-voltage, low-energy or halogen energy sources. For surface lighting you could use can-like downlighters, track-type spot lights or low-voltage lamps suspended on cables. This category also includes decorative centre and wall lights.

3 In this long room in Helsinki a group of vintage pendant lamps fill the void within the high ceiling. To find multiples of great lighting is a rare occurrence. **4** In this Brooklyn house a row of downlighters floods the floor below with halogen light. **5** Amongst the beams of this old school house low-hung pendants modernise the space.

Concealed lighting would give overall lighting in display areas, on stair cases and at strategic areas in the home, such as at different floor levels where the use of florescent lighting could be a good idea. Free-standing lighting includes table and floor lights. This type of lighting offers the opportunity to give atmosphere to the room. Whether you choose contemporary or vintage examples is your choice.

Throughout the 20th century there have been key examples of iconic lighting. In the 1930s the British Bestlite was featured in all the best interior and architecture magazines of the time. Available in a desktop, wall and floor-standing version it covered all needs. In the 1950s the

6 In a contemporary dining room within a Victorian terrace a mix of modern furniture and period lighting creates an individual style. **7** Two types of lighting illuminate this small home office. The uplighter will flood the room with bright light while the contemporary crystal pendant will create an intimate atmosphere. **8** Suspended in mid air, this zeppelin-type pendant floats beneath the Victorian rose in the entrance of this San Francisco town house. **9** With all this daylight a great deal of electric light is needed to compensate when the sun goes down. Here six pendants are suspended at random heights from the beamed ceiling.

George Nelson Bubble lamp hung from the best ceilings throughout the United States. In the 1970s the Arco lamp arched over various arrangements around the world. Now with so many classic modern designs being reproduced and re-introduced to the market the options are vast when it comes down to what lamp to choose and where to display it

With directional lighting, again the options are endless. With a vast array of fittings available, and an increasing number of sources, ranging from the local DIY store to the architectural lighting specialist, there is something for every budget. Whether you opt for the low-voltage or angled downlighter, the flood lamp or the recessed spot lamp, it is really up to you to select the correct installation for your space.

10 Angled to mirror the beams, this Italian production task lamp is ideal for bedtime reading as it swivels and tilts wherever you may need it.
11 This grouping of architectural paper lamps by Noguchi fills a corner of this Brooklyn townhouse. As well as bringing light when needed they bring a timeless atmosphere to this family room.

DISPLAY

If you have something to show, why not have it on display? To create an area purely for display is an instant way to make your interior an individual one and inject personality. Whatever you may collect, whether it be books, pots, African art, 1970s glass or 1980s Barbie dolls, to have them on display will make the atmosphere of the room or space.

Getting the balance right is the clever part. A whole room dominated by glassware can be too much, but one alcove of it can be a great backdrop to your other stuff. Deciding how and where to make your display area can be the tricky part. Of course you want the arrangement to be in a place where you are going to appreciate it, but is also needs to be located in an area that is not better utilised for something else, more useful – for the television and sound system, for example. How you should house your display is another challenge to be solved. You can buy various units of furniture specifically designed for this,

1 On this rosewood chest by George Nelson is a well-grouped selection of family heirlooms and flea-market finds. On the wall hangs a new work by Jo Shane. **2** These items have just happened to arrive here. Containing a selection of items within a tray or frame creates an instant display. **3** Behind the sinuous deSede sofa a shelf runs the length of the room, enabling a constant change of artworks Here a mix of photography and other media are on view.

4 In the lobby area between the living and bedroom areas in this house in Sarasota, Florida, a group of ethnic and tribal art looks tempting. The massive shelf is built into the alcove walls.

5 In the kitchen, display is often forgotten. Decorative vessels look good on display even without the fruit they might sometimes hold. The items here all carry a pierced element as a linking theme. **6** Chainstore shelves are fixed up above a bed at different spacings. This arrangement enables many permutations of display. Here paintings, pottery and baskets are put together.

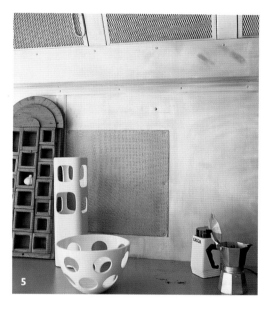

whether it be a series of shelves for an alcove or along a wall or a complete free-standing unit with individual sections to divide and categorise the collection.

I always feel that a mixed selection of items looks best. Include books, some art objects and artefacts – maybe even integrate the various parts of your hi-fi system as well so as to make it look less obvious, and as though your collection has grown and developed over the years. Having a mixture of items makes the display less precious and more approachable for your guests and visitors to appreciate.

Other elements will have to be taken into consideration. Lighting, for example, is an important part of a good display area – whether you use spot-type lights or illuminate with concealed lighting depends on your own ideas. Directional spots give you more flexibility as you can angle the lamp on

your favourite pieces. With concealed lighting you can usually back light the whole arrangement, which in itself can visually become a focal point to the room.

In some cases a whole room can be called a display, especially if you collect classic furniture. A group of key pieces of 1950s furniture in the right setting is an instant collection on display. It may be a bit precious, but in an open-plan loft space this can work very well, as there will be enough space for useful seating arrangements.

It all depends on your level of obsession. Some of us are forever looking for the next object to add to the collection. So in those cases a flexible system would be more suitable. An area that perhaps has open and concealed areas is maybe best suited for this, so that you can have your favourite pieces on display and the others behind closed doors.

1 This unique idea, in a Victorian house in San Francisco, works as a book store and also a balustrade to the staircase that sweeps down behind it. The units are suspended between a light steel structure. **2** In this white room, storage on wheels is a flexible solution. You can wheel it to the utility room when you run out of clean clothes. **3** In a house in Sarasota, Florida, which has been extended by Guy Peterson, an entire wall is given over to cubby holes for the gathering of favourite books and objects. This area is not an arranged display; it is a forever changing full-height backdrop to the room.

With the clutter-free, minimalist interior inspiring most of our choices in our home today, storage has to be the most important element to make the modern lifestyle function effectively. Think about where you are going to need storage, what it is to be used for and how often you will need to access it. The choice of either open or closed storage, and for built-in or free-standing storage units all depends on the surroundings in which they will sit.

Storage problems are solved so simply. With the off-the-shelf systems so easily available from most of the chain stores, you can buy a complete wall of storage and take it away with you that day. Of course, you can get the carpenters in to do this and that, but why bother when you can get the ideal system so reasonably? Using existing alcoves for storage seems like an obvious

4 In the small hallway is this Helsinki apartment full-height cupboards have been installed. Although quite shallow they can still contain many items. **5** In the entrance lobby to a loft space in New York this complete wall of veneered panels disguises both deep walk-in storage and regular racked-out closets. **6** Understair storage is often hard to access. With both pull-out and open-up storage, here every square inch is usable.

solution, but to use a complete wall of storage units as a divide between two existing areas is an advanced idea and utilises your space to the full. Those of us who live in a reclaimed industrial space without the usual domestic framework appreciate the importance of good storage.

The items you are storing will dictate the type, size and scale of storage you are installing. You could have concealed fixings to doors so that the area looks like a flat wall. You could have a grid of small doors to make the whole wall of openings look more decorative. The doors could be timber fronted or veneer-faced board; they could be painted to match or to contrast or they could be glass.

Open storage can look good when combined with groupings of display items. Using free-standing storage units can work well if they are the correct proportion and style for the room. Using vintage pieces especially can give a great feel to the room as well as being useful. A long sideboard will provide both storage within the cupboards and display space on top. One of the many combined storage systems

7 In a house with this addition by Guy Peterson in Sarasota, Florida, the plasma screen is mounted above a custom-built metal-clad unit that pulls out and opens up and houses all the entertainment equipment. To add to its architectural feel, the top of the unit is fashioned out of a slab of concrete. **8** The entertainment in this London house is instantly available to use or it can be hidden when not needed. It is concealed by walnut-faced sliders. **9** A long low sideboard is available for storage, but also doubles up as a great surface for display. Above hangs a pair of identical mirrors. **10** To use a partition as storage is an ingenious way to break up a space; behind this wall of closets in the bathroom is the master bedroom.

dating from the mid-20th century can solve a great deal of problems, with a unit that includes open shelving, drawers, drop-flap cupboards and even a desk area.

When you look at room with storage in mind always try to work out your furniture layout first. You may deprive yourself of valuable wall space if you have pieces that need to stand against a wall or if you have favourite artwork you want to hang in a prominent place. Organising your lifestyle and clearing out all unwanted items is the way forward. Storage should be discreet and exploit areas that are not good for other uses. You could use the space under the bed, you could disguise the ugly boxed-in areas for the boiler and flue by including it within a larger storage unit. You could use the eaves of the roof for a wall of recessed storage.

FURNITURE AND FURNISHINGS

One of the easiest and quickest ways to make your home more modern is to update your furniture and furnishings. This could be an instant transformation, such as updating your old sofa with a new cover in a great colour or print or putting up new window coverings.

In a rental situation some of the furniture you inherit with the lease can be pretty basic. But with a bit of time and money, that old seating arrangement could be transformed into the ideal relaxation area with a few modern pillows and a textured throw – how easy is that?

In a more traditional home, perhaps a Victorian terrace, the placing of good-looking items of furniture can be a great balance to the original features of an older house. A really good piece of 1920s design – the Barcelona chair by Mies van der Rohe, for example – can gel surprisingly naturally against a moulded and panelled fire surround.

2

1 Furniture, as well as being comfortable, has to look good. The Arne Jacobsen egg chair, here covered in hide, gives the added curves to this otherwise linear interior. **2** Custom-made furniture does in most cases solve the problem of finding the right piece for the right place and making sure it does the job required. This low-level deck for the plasma screen does not interfere with the window feature in this room.

3 On a deep shag-pile rug, the classic Noguchi coffee table makes a sculptural statement. **4** You do not need the originals to create the right interior. Here, in a mid-fifties house, reissues of furniture by George Nelson, particularly the day bed, have been used. The amoebic table softens the hard corners. **5** A see-through chair by Bertoia needs a pillow for added comfort, while its graphic qualities are inviting.

Choosing furniture can be a lengthy and tedious task. Before you buy it is better to try to experience the space for a while until you have worked out how you use it and made a list of your requirements. The size of the sofa, the type of dining table, the colour of the rug and the window treatments: these are all the sorts of decision you will need to come to once you have assessed your needs.

In your space it is the selection of the furniture and furnishings that make it your home. Throughout the world the desire for modern styling has been so great that many classic pieces of modern design are so widely reproduced, some by the original manufacturers and some by the firms that do various versions of the original. If you simply want to create a look, the non-original versions are ideal,

6 The Le Corbusier Basculant chair always looks good, wherever you put it. Designed in the 1920s, it is hard to believe it still looks so modern. In this library its framework relates to the uprights of the book shelves.

7 Poul Kjaerholm chairs are classics from the mid 1950s. Their streamlined profile works well in any material. These chairs also come in leather or canvas. The table is by Mies van der Rohe.

8 In this classically proportioned room the Bull chair by Arne Jacobsen hovers in the wings. In the room there is an eclectic mix of styles, creating an individual style, but every piece relates to the next. **9** The plastic stacking storage system by Anna Castelli has recently been reissued, making a visual and useful bedside cabinet. The chair keeps the circular theme going.

8

as they do look good. But they do lose their value as soon as you buy them. If you are going to buy classic pieces of furniture as an investment, make sure you buy them direct from the original manufacturer. These pieces will certainly retain, or increase, their value.

There is so much good new design around now that whatever you are looking for there is a wide range of price and quality to choose from. From Scandinavian chairs to the American original manufacturers, you can select from a vast array of good design. A mix of both is a clever way to do it. Get your key elements of storage and display from the chain stores and select a few iconic pieces from the top manufacturers.

New design around these days relates so much to original pieces that perhaps if you do not have the time to select good vintage pieces, non-original modern examples are the best option for you. There are many sources, but maybe working with a good furniture and design dealer is the way of getting what you really want.

I believe it is always a good thing to try to find less obvious pieces of design, perhaps from the lesser known, but still great, designers. The way forward is to include key modern pieces in your interior, whether original or reproduction. On the whole its the look that counts.

Of course, condition also matters. In a minimal, clutter-free environment, the last thing you want is a worn-out piece of furniture, but in an ecclectic, ex-industrial space it would look fine.

Together with good design, good condition and with the furniture well placed within the space, the modernised home will be complete.

ZONES FOR MODERN LIVING

The zones for modern living reflect the activities we carry out in our homes, and to which in traditional homes completely separate rooms are devoted – they are obviously for relaxing, cooking and eating, sleeping, bathing and working. Which ones you develop is up to you. If you are working on a space new to you and you are living in it at the same time, you have to decide on your priorities. If you work from home you may need to get that space established first and foremost so that you can get back to work as soon as you can. If you can work elsewhere you may want to get the basics, such as plumbing and electrical works, done first.

It is perhaps more commonplace to get all the services in place as soon as you can, but sometimes it is hard to make decisions without having first experienced the space properly If you are looking to modernise your existing home, at least you have had time to think about what you really need from the space. Is the bathroom in the right place? Does the kitchen layout work for you? Is there enough storage in the relaxing area? Do you want an ensuite shower room? Will you need more drastic alterations such as stripping out or moving walls? It all really takes time to work out.

Modernisation through changing or updating decorative features produces less disruption and as you are not doing any structural work many zones can be worked on at once. Getting a new floor laid throughout the zones, for example, will unite them and instantly transform them.

The choice of which zones to develop and when is a personal one. To some a great relaxing zone is more important than the cooking zone. If you have no desire or urge to be a master chef why waste time and money creating a super kitchen if you are not going to use it? If you do not work from home.just make sure you have some space for the home computer. Of course the sleeping and bathing zones need to work in any home, but there are simple and cost-effective ways to work on these areas. In both spaces storage is always important. Somewhere to put things can only add to the benefits of modernising your home.

Breaking the home up into zones makes it easier to work on one area at a time, even though you do not want to treat them as individual spaces. You want one to flow to the next. You want them to be, on the whole, flexible and you want them to enhance your everyday modern lifestyle.

RELAXING ZONE

One of the most valued assets of having your own space is to be able to create the most relaxing areas you can within your own home. To be able to come home from work, or to have finished working at home and moving into or settling into the relaxing zone is the most important part of living in, and enjoying, a modern home.

This home must do all you want it to do. But creating a zone to chill out in is perhaps not a simple task. There are many aspects of the relaxing zone to consider, such as the colours and patterns to be used, the type of decoration and even the introduction of built-in furniture.

Within the home the relaxing zone really needs the most thought as it will be used for so many different activities. If you are just doing a quick make-over of this space – purely decorative modernisation – all you are really going to consider is the colour and decoration, the flooring and other surface finishes and perhaps new or updated furniture to work within the improved space.

The decoration in the relaxing zone needs to be cool and calm, but perhaps with a focal element of pattern or other colour to give it a personality. You do not really want it to be too stark and organised as this is the zone where you will be entertaining most probably, where you will be reading the Sunday papers and perhaps where the children will play. A little bit of visual clutter can sometimes make the room. You will need storage areas, display areas, space for the television and sound systems and, of course, comfortable seating.

If you are going to start to update the features of the home, you may want to remove an existing fireplace so that the television screen can go in its place, you may want to remove a dividing wall to give you more space to relax in or

I In this In this mid 1950s Florida home, walls of glass let the outside in, and increase the living space. Outdoor furniture also becomes as important as that selected for the interior.

2

2 The raised level of a former tram shed in Amsterdam makes an ideal place for an area to relax in. Away from the service areas of the space, the grouping looks appealing. **3** The L-shaped house allows for a second, more intimate sitting area. With a wall of entertainment equipment this area is ideal for the kids or the grown-ups. The low-level table and all those pillows encourage the use of the rug for extra seating. **4** In the roof-top room in this New York loft a glamorous sectional sofa zig-zags around the room. Facing the windows, it gives a great outlook onto the New York skyline.

you may want to install an entire wall of dedicated storage to house all the unsightly entertainment equipment.

Re-organising this space could give you grander solutions. Besides removing a wall you might want to totally configure the layout of the main floor of your home so as to create a more open-plan space for relaxing in. To make a flowing plan from one space to another, and perhaps linking this space to the cooking and eating zone and maybe even the working zone will create an ideal environment for 21st-century living.

The ultimate in making a relaxing zone stand out from the rest would be if you were to extend your space to create a great light-filled room, that went out into the garden space, that included an outdoor sitting and relaxing zone and that naturally continued the flow of the house outside.

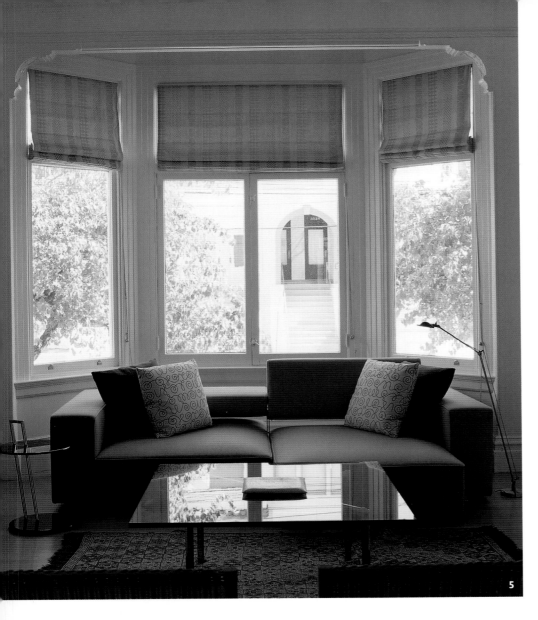

5 The bay window in this room is in a good position for the sofa. This wide one houses a seating arrangement that has moveable elements so each user can create their ideal sitting position. The window can be closed off with Roman blinds to create a more cosy atmosphere. **6** This space is one total chill-out zone. With the mix of shapes, colour and graphics the entire interior is visually stunning. The long low seating element allows for group entertaining.

The important thing to consider if you are building an extension to your home for this reason is that it is accessible, that it has a purpose and that it is inviting to both the eye and the body and, of course, the inevitable comfort it can give.

Whatever way you decide to modernise your home the furniture and furnishings you select for this zone must work. Whether you update what you have with new coverings and finishes, whether you just add new window treatments or whether you just add bold cushions or a wacky carpet, these are all important elements for this space.

Relaxing comfortable seating does seem to be the most difficult item to find. There are many great-looking sofas available, but are they comfortable? The seating units are on the top of the list when selecting furniture for the relaxing zone. Do you want vintage or contemporary, sectional or conventional? Its up to you. If you have a good comfortable seating arrangement already perhaps the best thing to do is to have it re-upholstered in a new colour or more modern fabric. If you are buying new, test drive as much as you can. Maybe a friend has a great-looking sofa? Try it out. But even if you are stuck with your old faithful sofa, a new batch of patterned cushions can add that bit of extra visual and physical comfort you have been looking for.

The relaxing zone might also include your eating or working place. These areas have to gel with the main space, and not interfere with the overall effect. By using similar or complementary styles, fabrics and colours you can create a space of harmony and relaxation. The relaxing zone must be seriously considered: it has to be inviting, accommodating and work for you, your friends and your family.

6

SLEEPING ZONE

The eight hours of sleep we require a night needs to be experienced in the appropriate setting. Whether you are creating bedtime quarters for yourself, your children or your occasional guests, the sleeping zone is so much more than simply a bed placed in a room.

When you are deciding how to modernise your home, the sleeping areas are perhaps the ones to consider first. After all, getting a good night's sleep will get you through the next stage of development and also give you time to mull over decisions. Not that you need have sleepless nights while working on your home, but I find it is often at night when great ideas occur. I always keep a pad and pencil next to my bed to jot things down or sketch a layout or fitting detail.

So the space could be for yourself, your children or maybe an office-come-guest room. These days, with our flexible ways of living, we always seem to need to incorporate so many other things into our rooms. In the bedroom, beside the bed we need ample storage for clothes, adequate areas for television and entertainment equipment, a mini library, good lighting for night-time reading, perhaps a small work area, an area for the fitness equipment if you are that way inclined and then, maybe, if there is enough space, an ensuite bathroom.

This is just in your room. If you are working on a child's room you will need much more storage for toys as well as clothes, more flexible sleeping arrangements for a sleepover

1 This bedroom opens onto a wraparound terrace that overlooks San Francisco Bay. To wake up and experience this view must be exceptional as it is ever changing through the seasons and the times of the day and night. **2** In the centre of this space is the bed. This sleeping zone is also extra seating when entertaining and is used by the owners to watch their favourite television shows This arrangement calls for strict organisation.

3 The windows of this bedroom resemble artworks hanging on the wall. With the tropical outlook you know where you are. The built-in bed and side units keep the room well organised and easy to maintain. **4** In the centre of this mews house, one of the bedrooms has high-level glass panels to let light in. Used as an occasional bedroom, it is divided from the next room by a small shower room. Note the flush ceiling speakers for total ambience.

and a suitable area to do the homework. In the guest room, a sofa bed or one that folds into the wall keeps the space more useful for other activities such as the home office.

All of these are key elements of the installation of a sleeping zone. The decoration of these areas is also as important. As in the relaxing zone, colour and pattern are important. In this zone it all depends how you like to sleep – you are, after all, creating this space for yourself. Some like to be in total darkness while others like to be woken by bright white morning light. This of course can be controlled by the appropriate window treatments, but on the whole, when keeping or making your home modern a brighter decor is the ideal solution. You can darken it when you want to sleep and brighten it up when you need to wake.

Going back to the basics, the bed of course needs to right for you, your sleeping patterns and your personal preferences as to a hard or soft mattress. It also depends on the size of the space you have designated for this zone. With such a wide range of sleeping products available there is something for everyone and every budget – whether you choose a twin, queen or king size bed, it's all up to you. It is what else you introduce into this zone that will make this space modern and personal to you.

If you are looking for the quickest and simplest way of modernisation the use of great fabrics and paints can make your zone comprehensively more modern. The decoration is what you will initially see and it will create the atmosphere and ambience of the room. To create extra storage you could use the space under the bed. You can fix a television onto a wall-hung mechanism, you can add new bedcovers and window treatments and you can hang new lamps. All of these are simple projects that are quick to complete.

Updating the more permanent features of the sleeping zone would include replacing old-fashioned doors on wardrobes and storage with new streamlined or even mirrored alternatives, installing a new ambient lighting system or even remove a redundant fireplace and use this for the entertainment storage area. Of course, whatever way you may modernise, the floor in the sleeping zone is a very

5 A headboard with all the works: lighting and ample storage keeps this space tidy. **6** Amongst the beams of this Victorian space a low-level bed looks inviting. While the massive timbers could dominate this space the fact that everything else is close to the floor brings your eye level down.

7

7 In the roof space of an old factory a skylight brings in ample light. Built-in storage runs the length of the old beam under the eaves while vintage drawer units by Florence Knoll house the smalls. **8** In this tiny room the bed runs along one wall. The custom-built headboard accentuates the height of the room, as do the wall applique set at a low level. The pillows and shag-pile rug adds cosiness.
9 Here a collection of mid-20th-century furniture is grouped. The headboard, night stand and drawer unit are all by George Nelson, as is the book shelf at the end of the bed. Designed in the early 1950s, it couldn't be any more modern. The chair in the foreground is by Ralph Rapson.

8

important element. To step out onto a rough sisal floor or a soft sheepskin rug is all a matter of personal taste, but in this zone it is often overlooked.

If you are in the situation of reorganising your space then you can really go to town about getting everything you need in this space. Using a wall of storage to divide the sleeping zone from the bathing zone is a great way to get over storage problems in both zones. A sleeping platform could be included by raising or lowering floors. If you have a chance of extending into your roof space, this is perhaps a good time to create the ultimate sleeping zone. Being able to use one floor of your home for this personal zone would create a luxurious area that includes a bath area and all the requirements you associate with this zone.

Whatever way you modernise your home, in this zone the constraints are much the same: to create a suitable area to sleep, to be a retreat from the outside world and make a private space within a sociable home.

9

BATHING ZONE

1 In this bathroom designed by Anne Fougeron for her own use, she has created a place you want to spend time in. With its glazed roof and wall you are enclosed, with the elements outside and above.

In the home the bathing zone could be ensuite, a shower room, a family bathroom, a wet room or it could be a steam room or include a jacuzzi. What you ideally want and what you end up with does, of course, depend on the space you have and your budget. It also depends on your plumbing facilities and your overall needs in your home.

In the bathroom you need privacy, so the positioning of it within the total scheme is very important. If you are just decorating or updating for a more modern feel you will probably have to put up with the existing placing of this room. But if the bathroom is on a level away from the bedrooms, or using too large a space, relocating is understandable. You can now though quite easily relocate wet areas using a macerator that uses a very small pipe for waste. But to do this work is unnecessary unless your existing facilities are very inconvenient.

2 A suspended mirror screens off the bath. It houses a concealed light. It also opens up for ample storage. The sink unit is made from stainless steel. Overall the walls are covered with sheet glass. **3** The towel store is faced with very thin laminate marble which creates a translucent panel which is illuminated at night. More stainless steel has been used for low-level storage, while the floor is poured terrazzo.

4

5

Today there is so much to choose from in the bathroom market. There are space-saving systems, built-in, free-standing and wall-hung bathtubs, basins and toilets that make the choices endless. I suppose one of the worst scenarios is that you inherit an oddly coloured bathroom from previous owner. This would have to go, unless you are brave and can work out a scheme to include and update it. If you are lucky enough to have a white suite, these can usually be cleaned up, whatever condition they are in, and new wall finishes, taps and accessories can easily and quickly make this zone sparkle. These days, with so many materials for wall finishes in wet areas available, there is no excuse for using the obvious. Even though most people's preference is to have a white suite with white tiles a bit of imagination can create a personalised space.

If you are reorganising or extending your home the placing of the bathroom or rooms can be up to you. To create an ensuite wet area in a small unit can

4 In a bathroom in a house in London by Curtis Wood architects different levels – the bench, the sink unit and the storage unit – give ample space for a family bathroom. The timber used in this wet room needs regular maintenance to protect its surface. **5** A special paint finish has been used on the plaster walls that makes them totally waterproof. The floor has a hidden gully to take away the shower water. Above is a glass panel that brings light into this top-floor room. **6** In the second bathroom, a free-standing bathtub has been installed. While a shower is ideal for everyday use sometimes we need a soak.

save space. But you may also need a separate cloakroom to avoid having guests traipse through your bedroom. If you have a family you will obviously need a family bathroom as well. If you have two wet areas these can be back to back or side by side to save on plumbing costs. They look better if they are treated the same, with the same fittings and tiles or wall finishes. You could always use different towels and accessories to make them more suitable for the family.

The bathing zone should also carry on some sort of theme from the main living space. Use the same type or size of tile or designer taps as in the kitchen, for example. Use the same lighting as in the hallway, or the main bedroom when installing an ensuite and perhaps include similar built-in storage as in the bedroom or dressing area so as to unit the spaces. The idea is to create a natural flow from

6

7   **8**

one space to another. Using similar colour flooring, from timber to tile, also visually unites the space.

An extension could create an amazing bathing zone or wet space. You can build a box specifically as a bathroom with perhaps no windows but with skylights, with sunken areas for shower waste or with central drainage so the entire space becomes a shower room. You could also create a room with a view, so that you can bathe without being overlooked or so that you look out over the bay or across the roof tops.

If you have children, you need to take them into consideration when working out the layout, scale of fittings and the type of taps that need

to be easy to use and easy to maintain. Bathrooms are an area of the home that are, no matter how well fitted out and decorated, often redone when a new owner comes along. The tiles are either the wrong colour, there is a bath and you want a shower or vice verse, or in some cases it is in the wrong place. So when working on this zone plan it with yourself in mind and make sure it works for you.

The bathing zone is an important part of today's home. It has to be private, yet work for your family and guests. It has to function well, with good water pressure for showers, and you need space to store all those bathroom and beautifying products.

7 This bathroom has totally opaque sliding windows, so there is no need for blinds or other window treatments. The mosaic wall adds great colour to the space and its compactness shows good planning. **8** Here a tiny bathroom has been squeezed between two bedrooms. The shape of the strip window is exaggerated by the use of the strip storage unit and shelf below. All the wall surfaces are painted. The toilet is wall mounted to increase the visual floor space. **9** The glass wall in this shower room has been sand blasted on the lower two thirds for privacy, so you can shower and look out at the view without being noticed.

COOKING AND EATING ZONE

The kitchen is the most frequently updated and modernised zone of the house. One person's ideal is not always shared by the next man.

In the home, the kitchen and eating areas are now often included within the main hub of the house. An open-plan space is usually worked around a central cooking and eating area, making this area a dividing space between the communal and private of the home. The simplest way to modernise or update this zone is to work with what you have. If you have good cabinets, update the doors, refresh the splashback and put in new taps. All of this can be done quickly and easily and would cause little disruption. You can even update the appliances to a new finish or get integral versions that go behind closed doors. If you have culinary ambitions, perhaps you could rearrange the kitchen to cater for them. You can get industrial-looking stoves now for the domestic market that suit these needs. This is maybe too extreme for a regular domestic kitchen but it is an option if you intend to give this area heavy-duty use.

A cooking and eating zone should include ample work spaces for food preparation and for serving. It should have adequate appliances for your needs, the right size oven, the correct amount of hot plates, one or maybe two dishwashers (one for clean dishes, one for dirty) and ample storage for cooking utensils and for food, both of the refrigerated and larder type.

1 A well-stacked industrial shelf is the sign of a good cook, with a pot for every method of cooking.
2 In this Amsterdam home an industrial kitchen has been installed. On open island incorporates storage and an eating area and also houses a set-in sink.
A wall of locker-type cabinets adds to the storage elements while racks around the stove keeps everything at hand.

3 This open-plan kitchen has a bank of cupboards that protrude from the wall to form a peninsula unit. The simple white-painted units have a douglas fir worktop that relates to other timber elements found in the house. This kitchen leads to the central hallway. **4** The worktop has an in-set sink with a hob opposite. The wall cabinets hover just above the three-sided unit.

6

5 An overhang has been allowed here to create an area for entertaining and somewhere to sit for a well-earned break. **6** In this kitchen designed for an active cook an L-shaped island has been installed to give ample and necessary work surfaces. The reconstituted worktop offers a seamless and hygienic area for food preparation.

It is better if you can locate washing and drying services in their own dedicated area, but in this day and age space can be at a premium so if these functions have to be included in the kitchen there are clever decorative ways of integrating them within the cooking and eating zone.

To incorporate dining into this cooking space can mean that you need a breakfast bar area or a nearby dining table. You also will need storage for serving dishes and tableware, glasses and linens. The open-plan layout is good for the easy living ways of today. But of course if you are cooking in the

7 In a New York loft this grown-up kitchen, with its timber-faced units and exposed brick walls, makes the most of the bare materials of the old building. **8** The dining area in the same loft is in the central area of the space. The atrium nearby brings in light from above and adds another eating area, this time outside. The glass table top does somewhat allow it to disappear.

middle of the living area you will need a very powerful extractor hood to remove all cooking fumes at source.

Today, the more formal dining room has been taken over by a more relaxed arrangement. Even though the set up of a dining table and chairs does look good within the home, to give an entire room over to this is not the way forward. A more casual approach to eating has come into our lives and in some cases this table arrangement becomes a work table during the day and a dining table at night.

If you are reorganising your space this cooking/eating zone can be located anywhere. If you position it towards the centre of the space it means you can access it from all areas and it truly becomes the heart of your home. But it is also good to have this relaxing or eating zone opening directly onto an outdoor space, as this will increase the usable space considerably during the summer months.

The layout of the cooking area does depend on the space available. I always like to create some kind of island for the main appliances and sink areas. I find that when you have guests you can get a great group of friends around this space and it also makes an ideal location for serving food and drinks. Adding a couple of stools at the correct height will also make this island a casual eating area.

Then it comes down to the style and look of the zone. For me, a plain simple kitchen with white doors and worktops with concealed appliances and integral sink gives a timeless classic modern kitchen area that will sit happily within any open-plan environment, whatever the style ethos. If you want to personalise this basic palette, or pick up on themes used elsewhere in the adjoining spaces, you can add colour and texture with the careful choice of appliances and the occasional designer accessory.

9

10

Lighting in these zones is also very important. A well-illuminated cooking area is obviously needed, with concealed lighting above the cooktop. An extractor fan will maybe include lighting as well. A well-lit kitchen area is usually desirable, but it is great to have a dimmer to give ambient light at night after the cooking is done – you do not want to floodlight the dirty dishes. In the dining area a great vintage pendant lamp can make the space, and well-directed concealed spot lights can also create a great atmosphere.

The furniture selected for this area is just a matter of personal taste and style. Going for completely modern may mean going to the chain stores for great reasonably priced design, trawling through thrift stores or antique centres for good vintage examples or going straight to the top designers for good new iconic pieces, perhaps specially commissioned.

The cooking eating zone is the hub of the house, it needs to work, to be visually exciting and it needs to be modern.

9 In this high-ceilinged kitchen, the glass doors of the wall cabinets mean everything is on display. Every cupboard needs to be well thought out and contain interesting items, while the glass doors need to be spotless. If you are not this well organised, perhaps too much display might not be a good thing! **10** The central island always works well, especially if enough space is allowed around it. In this kitchen there is ample space for a dining arrangement of tables, long benches and chairs between the island and the staircase. **11** In this wide bay window, built-in seating creates a space-conscious dining area.

WORKING ZONE

At home we are working more and more. From our home office we are designing magazine layouts, making one-off handbags and writing books. The home–work space has firmly made its mark on our day-to-day living. It is now such a part of 21st-century living that it has to be included, these days, in all schemes we are working on.

Today working from home is commonplace. Whether you use the space under the stairs, an alcove in the main living area or a recess in the hallway it is a value-added asset. and whichever way you modernise your home, the workspace needs to be included. To have a spare room that you can turn into a home office is a real luxury. To have a small area of your home that you can make into an work space is still a bonus. There is no real need to have this space hidden, but sliding partitions around it that enable you to hide the work chaos is somewhat of a relief when you have guests.

These days there are many ways to create the home office zone. Using vintage storage, you may be able to use part of a wall unit for your desk and computer components. At home I have a small mezzanine floor that I use as a library and workspace. Books in the home are usually the biggest and heaviest bulk of stuff we have and display, so to build or install an appropriate place for books and magazines is very important. To include this in a working zone is ideal. It is surprising how much stuff we do hoard.

As time goes by, I'm sure we will be working from home more and more, as this culture becomes more deeply entrenched. The space taken up for the home office will at least double and the amount of time spent in the home will surely increase. The end of the 20th century saw this slowly happening; in this century more and more people are looking for quality of life and working from home just adds to this.

1 In the corridor of this Florida house endless sliding doors closet a hideaway office. It's there when you need it, invisible when you don't.
2 Karim Rashid's New York home–work area is basically a laptop on a glass table. This is as simple as it can be, but he includes other items such as good lighting and a sound system.

3 This office is divided from the main living space by a wall of storage on one side and a sliding partition on the other, which allows it to be closed off when neccessary.

SUPPLIERS

Most of the locations in this book include custom-built kitchens, storage and, in some cases, furniture. Suppliers for whom only a web sites address is given will supply locally. Some suppliers are trade only, but they will supply information if requested.

FLOORING

TIMBER BOARDS, STRIP PARQUET
www.junckers.com
01376 534700
Wide range of plank and strip flooring

www.1926woodflooring.com
2 Daimler Close
Royal Oak, Daventry
Northamptonshire NN11 8QJ
0870 5872027
Ranging from timber to bamboo and other laminates

Solidfloor
53 Pembroke Road
London W11
020 7221 9166
www.solidfloor.co.uk
Extensive range of traditional and exotic timbers

www.quick-step.com
Simple-to-lay laminated and solid flooring

Lassco Flooring
41 Maltby Street
London SE1
020 7237 4488
Reclaimed plank, strip and block flooring

PREFINISHED FACED PLYWOOD
James Latham Timber
Unit 4, Dolphin Way
Purfleet RM19 1NZ
01708 869800
www.lathamtimber.co.uk
Easy-to-lay prefinished birch-faced flooring panels

WOOD AND CONCRETE FLOOR PAINT
www.farrow-ball.com
01202 876141
Historic range of paints for walls, exteriors and floors

John Oliver
33 Pembridge Road
London W11 3HG
020 7221 6466
www.johnoliver.co.uk
Manufacturers of a good range of colours

STONE

Limehouse Gallery
Arch 47, South Lambeth Road
London SW8 1SS
020 7735 8555
www.limehousegallery.co.uk
Wide range of stone for walls and floors

Stone Age
19–23 Filmer Road
London SW6 7BU
020 7385 7954
Wide range of various stone and marble
for walls and floors

BRICK
www.ibstock.co.uk
0870 9034000
Manufacturers of bricks for walls
and floors

Chelwood Brick.
www.thebrickbusiness.co.uk
Longstanding manufacturers with wide
range

TERRAZZO
www.terrazzoireland.co.uk

FLOOR LAYERS AND POLISHERS
M&T Alpha Ltd
Unit 2, Munro Drive
Cline Road, London N11 2LZ
020 8368 2230
Terrazzo restorers and polishers

CARPET
www.carpetinfo.co.uk
Carpet manufacturers and suppliers in the
UK

Crucial Trading.
The Plaza, 535 Kings Road
London SW10
020 7376 7100
www.crucial-trading.com
Natural flooring for many installations

www.brintons.net
Modern runners and fitted carpets

RUGS
Christopher Farr
6 Burnsall Street
London SW3 3ZJ
020 7349 0888
www.cfarr.co.uk
New design rug manufacturers

The Rug Company
124 Holland Park Avenue
London W11 4UE
020 7229 5148
www.therugcompany.org
Art on the floor – modern rug design

STAIRCASES

Bisca
Sawmill Lane, Helmsley
North Yorkshire YO62 5DQ
01439 771702
www.bisca.co.uk.
Architectural staircases in glass and steel

www.jeld-wen.co.uk
0870 1260000
Timber staircase componets and off-the-
shelf designs

www.eyou.biz
Eyou Ltd/Stairsystems
Sterling House, Second Avenue
Chatham, Kent ME4 5AU
Spiral and kit staircases

DOORS AND WINDOWS

WOODEN CONSTRUCTION
Frank R Pratt
34 Plashet Grove, London E6
020 8472 0188
Custom-made windows and doors

METAL
www.steel-window-association.co.uk
Guide to various manufacters and restorers

Crittall Windows Ltd
Springwood Drive, Braintree
Essex CN7 2YN
01376 342106

www.crittall-windows.co.uk
Metal-frame windows and doors in various
styles, ranging from Georgian to Modernist

www.solaglas.co.uk
02476 547400
Large-scale sliding glass doors

Pollards Fyrespan
Haslemere Business Centre
Lincoln Way, Enfield
Middx EN1 1AY
020 8443 5511
Folding metal-frame doors

GLASS
Apropos
0870 3280033
Complete glass additions and extensions

www.drservices.co.uk
01992 447122

ROOF WINDOWS/SKYLIGHTS
www.velux.co.uk

WINDOWS FOR ROOFS
www.visiongroup.com.uk
01842 15581

SKYLIGHTS AND ROOF GLAZING
PC Henderson Ltd
Durham Road, Bowburn
Durham, DH6 5NG
01913 770701
www.pchenderson.com
Sliding-door gear and mechanisms

FIREPLACES

CVO Firevault
36 Great Titchfield Street
London W1W 8BQ
020 7580 5333
www.cvofirevault.co.uk
Architectural fireplace installations

Chesneys
194–202 Battersea Park Road
London SW11 4ND
020 7627 1410
www.chesneys.co.uk
Period to modern, repro or custom made

LIGHTING

www.erco.com
38 Dover Street, London W1
020 7408 0320
www.erco.com
Downlighters, track and architectural
lighting

www.ikea.co.uk
All types from retro to concealed

www.louis-poulsen.dk
Re-issuers of classic Scandinavian designs

Artemide
90–92 Great Portland Street
London W1 7JY
020 7631 5200
www.artemide.com
New and re-issues of classic domestic
lighting

SKK
34 Lexington Street
London W1F OLH
020 7434 4095
www.skk.net
Light installations, architectural lighting

www.deltalight.co.uk
Architectural recessed lighting

Encapsulite International
Unit 17, Chartmoor Road
Leighton Buzzard
Bedfordshire LU7 4WG
01525 376974
www.encapsulite.co.uk
Recessed florescent lighting

London Lighting Company
135 Fulham Road
London SW3 6RT
020 7589 3612
Modern and classic domestic lighting

SCP
135–139 Curtain Road
London EC2A 3BX
020 7739 1869
www.scp.co.uk
Re-issues of the classics plus some
new designs

DISPLAY, SHELVING, STORAGE

www.ikea.co.uk
All aspects of storage, open and closed,
from free standing to built in

Vitsoe
72 Wigmore Street
London W1 2SG
020 7935 4968
www.vitsoe.co.uk
Wall-mounted storage designed by Dieter
Rams in 1960

Charles Page
61 Fairfax Road
London NW6 4EE
020 7328 98751
www.charlespage.co.uk
Off-the-shelf storage for bedrooms and
bathrooms

The Holding Company
241–5 Kings Road
London SW3 5EL
All aspects of storage from moveable
to fixed

WALLS

PAINT
www.dulux.co.uk

John Oliver
See Flooring

www.farrow-ball.com
See Flooring

TILE
www.toppstiles.co.uk
The largest range of tiles and accessories
in the UK

www.pilkington.co.uk
Tile manufacturers for wall or floor

www.taylortiles.co.uk
Large selection of more unusual tiles

Mosaic Workshop
Unit B, 443–449
Holloway Road
London N7 6LJ
020 7263 2997
Mosaics for floor or wall

GLASS
Lee Green Glass
282 Lee High Road
London SE12
0800 838074
www.leegreenglass.com
From shelving to curtain walls of glass,
all architectural installations

Rankins Glass Co.
Pearson Street
London E2
020 7729 4200
Suppliers of glass and mirrors

Preedy Glass
Lamb Works, North Road
London N7 9DP
020 7700 0377
www.preedyglass.com
Installers of all glazing aspects

STONE
www.blancdebierges.com
From spiral staircases to slabs and sets

Limehouse Gallery
See Flooring

Stone Age
See Flooring

BRICK/BLOCKWORK
www.brick.org.uk
Guide for all brick manufactures in the
UK

www.ibstock.co.uk
Brick manufacturers

FURNITURE

NEW
www.ikea.co.uk
New design, good basics

B&B Italia
250 Brompton Road, London SW3 2AS
020 7591 8111
www.bebitalia.co.uk
High-end sofa systems

Chaplins
477–507 Uxbridge Road
Pinner, Middx HA5 4JS
0208421 1779
www.chaplins.co.uk
Wide range of new design and re-
editions

Aram
110 Drury Lane, London WC2B 5SG
020 7557 7557
www.aram.co.uk
Occasional pieces to complete units

Inhouse
28 Howe Street, Edinburgh EH3 6TG
01312252888
www.inhouse.co.uk
Wide range of modern design elements

SCP
135–139 Curtain Road, London EC2A 3BX
020 7739 1869
Own range of modern furniture plus re-
editons from Scandinavia and the US

REPRODUCED AND ORIGINAL CLASSICS
www.cassina.it
Repros of classics by Corbusier, Mies
vander Rohe and Macintosh

www.modernica.net
Re-editons of Eames and Nelson designs

www.hermanmiller.com
Reproductions of Eames office furniture

Fritz Hansen
20–22 Rosebery Avenue, London EC1
020 7610 4196
www.fritzhansen.com
Re-issues of Arne Jacobsen and Poul
Kjareholm furniture

www.knoll.com
Re-issues of work by Florence Knoll,
Harry Bertoia and Saarinen

Geoffrey Drayton
85 Hampstead Road, London NW1 2PL
020 7387 5840
www.geoffrey-drayton.co.uk
Up-to-the-minute design plus some
classics

Habitat
196 Tottenham Court Road
London W1P 9LD
020 7631 3880
www.habitat.net
Re-issues by Robin Day

Skandium
86 Marylebone High Street
London W1
020 7935 2077
www.skandium.com
All the expected Scandinavian classics

www.centuryd.com
US and UK Design

www.1stdibs.com
Intenational website of many dealers

CUSTOM
Opus Magnum
313 Merton Road, London SW18 5JS
www.opusmagnum.co.uk
Custom-built storage

Bill Mostow
rumsky@hotmail.com
001 602 840 5647
Custom-made occasional and built-in
furniture

KITCHENS

www.corian.com
The best plain worktops for any
installation

www.formica-europe.com
Widest colour range available for coating
any kitchen or worktop

www.ikea.co.uk
Good basic carcasses for your own
customised doors

Bulthaup
37 Wigmore Street, London W1
020 7317 6010
www.bulthaup.com
Complete installation, with many free-
standing options

www.tsunami.com
Minimalist installations with maximum
cost

BATHROOMS

www.vola.com
Taps by Arne Jacobsen

CP Hart
Newnham Terrace, Hercules Road
London SE1 7DR
020 7902 1000
www.cphart.co.uk
Wide range of top range sanitary ware

Edwins
17,19 and 26 All Saints Road
London W11 1HE
020 72213550
Good range of up-to-date taps and
chinaware for the modern bathroom

www.kaldewei.com
Best range of plain simple baths

www.duravit.com
Wide range of state of the art bathroom
equipment and accessories

www.lefroybrooks.com
Traditional bathroom taps, showers and
accessories

www.boffi.com
Italian design for the bathroom

www.jacobdelafon.com
French range of baths and sanitary ware

ARCHITECTS

Ulla Koskinen
Untamonte 4a 00610
Helsinki
Finland
003 58986835450
koskinen.rantanen@sci.fi

MIKKO PUOTILA RESIDENCE, HELSINKI:
19 right, 93 right, 98 bottom left, 120 left,
122, 144, 145.
RITVA PUOTILA RESIDENCE, HELSINKI: *7 left, 52.*
NEILAMA RESIDENCE, HELSINKI:
20, 32, 33, 38, 118 right, 130 bottom left,
166 right.

Kari Lappalainen
003 5896801828
kari.lappalainen@pp7.inet.fi

ILLKA APARTMENT, HELSINKI:
98 bottom centre, 124 right, 140, 142
bottom right, 153 right, 153 left, 155 bottom
left,163.

Gene Leedy
555 Avenue G NW
Winter Haven
FL 33880
001 863 293 7173
www.geneleedyarchitect.com
001 863 293 7173

JUNIOR WHITTINGHILL RESIDENCE, FLORIDA:
10, 102 left, 176 bottom right, 177.
ROBERT KAISER RESIDENCE, FLORIDA:
50, 51, 118 centre, 123 right, 146, 147, 157.

Anne Fougeron
Fougeron Architecture
720 York St Suite 107
San Francisco
CA 94110
001 415 641 5744
anne@fougeron.com
www.fougeron.com

FOUGERON RESIDENCE SAN FRANCISCO:
6, 39 top left, 44, 45, 46, 47, 96 bottom
right, 114 left, 115 bottom left, 121, 130
right, 134 right, 138 left, 148, 149, 168, 169.

Curtis Wood Architects
Andrew Wood/Jason Curtis
The Shopfront
84 Haberdasher Street
London N1 6EJ
020 7684 1400
www.curtiswoodarchitects.com
info@curtiswoodarchitects.com

STARK RESIDENCE, LONDON:
3, 14, 54, 55, 56, 57, 73, 97 right, 103 left,
109 top right, 142 top right, 170, 171.

Andrew Weaving
modern@centuryd.com
www.centuryd.com
07808 727615

WEAVING/THOMASSON RESIDENCE, LONDON:
30, 31, 70, 71, 99, 102 right, 109 bottom
right, 155 top left,166 left, 172 right.
WEAVING/THOMASSON RESIDENCE, ESSEX:
21, 26, 82, 83, 84, 85, 96 top right, 112
right centre, 128, 167, 155 bottom right,
167, 176 top left, 176 bottom left.

Marc Prosman Architecten Bv
Overtoom 197
1054 Ht Amsterdam
31(0)204892099
Fax 31(0)204893658
architecten@prosman.ni
www.prosman.ni

VAN BREESTRAAT, AMSTERDAM:
1, 5, 7 centre, 60, 61, 62, 63, 95, 126, 158,
182 right.
ALBERDINGH THIJMSTRAAT, AMSTERDAM: *58,*
59, 97 left.
SURINAMPLEIN, AMSTERDAM: *93, 94, 112, 115*
top right,155 top right.

Next Architects
Weesperzijde 93
1091 Ek Amsterdam
31(0)20463 0463
Fax 31(0)203624745
info@nextarchitects.com
www.nextarchitects.com

DE STAD, AMSTERDAM:
123 bottom left, 152, 174, 175.
PRINCENGRACHT, AMSTERDAM:
153 centre.

Don Chapell (Deceased)
Guy Peterson Faia
Guy Peterson/Ofa Inc
1234 First Street
Sarasota
FL 34236
001 941 952 1111
www.guypeterson.com
guypeterson@guypeterson.com

FISHMAN RESIDENCE, FLORIDA:
8, 16, 19 left, 19 centre, 74, 75, 76, 77, 78,
79, 96 left, 104 right, 136, 139, 142 left,
164 left.
Interiors by Wilson Stiles, Sarasota, Florida.

Ogawa Depardon Architects
137 Varick Street No 404
New York
NY 10013

212 627 7390
Fax 212 627 9681
www.oda-ny.com

HOUSE IN BROOKLYN, NEW YORK:
13, 64, 65, 88, 89, 90, 91, 92, 129, 133, 135:
Interior By Michael Formica.
HILPERT RESIDENCE, SAN FRANCISCO:
12, 100, 101, 111, 114 top right, 114
bottom right, 116, 117, 125, 131, 143,
162, 173.
NIPON APARTMENT, NEW YORK:
18, 86, 87, 124 left.

Downtown Group
236 West 27th Street No 701
New York
NY 10001
212 675 9506
info@downtowngroup.com
www.downtowngroup.com

KANETELL RESIDENCE, NEW YORK:
2, 11, 80, 81, 106, 107, 118 bottom left,
141 left, 159 right, 178, 179.

1100architect.com
435 Hudson Street 8th Floor
New York
NY 10014
212 645 1011
Fax 212 645 4670
info@1100architect.com

SHANE/COOPER RESIDENCE, NEW YORK:
23 right, 28, 29, 53, 66, 67, 68, 69, 104
bottom left, 105, 134 left.
AND ALSO:
109 bottom left.

Karim Rashid
357 West 17th Street
New York
NY 10011
001 212 929 8657
info@karimrashid.com
www.karimrashid.com
KARIM'S OWN APARTMENT, NEW YORK:
22, 23 left, 24, 25, 161, 183.

Seibert Architects
Sam Holladay
352 Central Avenue
Sarasota
FL 34236
001 941 366 9161
www.seibertarchitects.com
Fax 941 365 0902

9, 103 bottom right, 114 top left, 115 top
left, 119 top left, 172 top left.

Others

GEORGE RESIDENCE:
Extension remodelling by Michael George
01225 850561
72, 93 centre, 112 bottom right, 120 right.

MANNISTO/POYHONEN APT, HELSINKI:
Interior by Tuula Poyhonen
tuula.poyhonen@fonet.fi
15, 34, 35, 89 top right,129 top left, 138
right.

LINCOLN/ORUM RESIDENCE, SUFFOLK:
Interior by Angi Lincoln
07957 621796
7 right, 36, 39 bottom left, 48, 49, 104 top
left, 109 top left, 113 left, 129 right, 132,
137 left, 165 right.

SPRINGMAN WESTOVER RESIDENCE, LONDON:
130 top left, 151.
HARDING RESIDENCE:
Architecture by Audrey Matlock Architects
180 left, 181 right.
MACKERETH/VOGEL RESIDENCE, LONDON:
Designed by Wells Mackereth
98 top left, 127, 180-181 centre.
COLLINS RESIDENCE, LONDON:
150.
RIOS RESIDENCE, LOS ANGELES:
110.
BOUCQUIAU RESIDENCE, BELGIUM:
Designed by Marina Frisenna
108 right.

INDEX

ACKNOWLEDGEMENTS

First of all I would like to thank Jacqui Small for having faith in this book idea and getting it off the ground during a not so easy time. Thanks to Kate John and Ashley Western for getting it all together and making a great job with the selection of locations and my garbled text.

Of course its the friends, clients, architects and designers who have made it so much easier and fulfilling, thanks to all of you. Being able to enter other people's homes, shuffle their possessions around and take over their lives for a day has made this book the way it is. To Angi and John and Antony and Eric – thanks for your patience and time. To Rob Bevan, I look forward to your new home, and thanks to Barbara and Mike George for letting us in, even though the job was not completed.

In the US, without the help, time and enthusiasm of Gilles Depardon, many of the pages in this book would be blank; also thank you Anne Fougeron for letting us in your home and for creating such a great photogenic house. In New York, thanks to Jo Shane and John Cooper for opening your doors to us. Many thanks to Karim Rashid for letting us free in your space. And of course in Florida, thanks initially to Martie Lieberman for putting up with my long-winded emails of questions and information! Without Martie, the great places in Sarasota would not have been so accessible. Thanks to Guy Peterson, Sam Holladay, and Junior Whittinghill and Robert Kaiser of Winter Haven. And of course, thanks so much to Les and Lois Fishman for your hospitality and time, we will be back!

In Finland, Ulla Koskinen ran around town showing us the great interiors featured here, promoting not only her own work but also that of the local competition, my thanks Ulla. In Amsterdam, Marc Prosman let us into at least three of his projects, all different, and all included here, thank you Marc. And thanks to Next Architects for organising access during our very short stay there.

Back home, thanks to Ian again for putting up with the paperwork, for being there before and after my trips and for just telling me to get on with it when necessary.